BORN
OR
MADE

Fear is a Liar. Defeat is Overrated.
Real Stories, Real Success.
An Entrepreneur's Guide to
Thriving in Business.

Larry G. Dix II

First edition

Advisor: Bridgetta Tomarchio
www.PlotTwistInk.com

PLOT·TWIST·INK

Published by Authors Unite Publishing

\\\ AUTHORSUNITE

DEDICATION

To all entrepreneurs, may you find mentors who inspire and challenge you as you grow on your own path. Remember that your journey is just as valuable as your destination.

TABLE OF CONTENTS

FOREWORD

by Marques Ogden

I am a former NFL Athlete, and I am the CEO of Ogden Ventures LLC, a media consulting company based in the Raleigh, North Carolina area. I have had the pleasure of knowing Mr. Larry Dix, the author of *Born or Made,* for many years now. Larry is one of the most brilliant, disciplined, hard-working individuals I know. He is full of wisdom and enlightenment and has a very good ability to connect with the people he is serving, which makes him an excellent person to learn from in terms of growing both personally and professionally!

Born or Made is a book anyone and everyone should read who is trying to elevate their game to the next level. This book will show you the strategies and action steps of some of the most successful people and how they achieved greatness in their lives. This book also unravels this age-old debate about whether super successful people are born with their skill sets or if they work hard to make themselves who they are.

Born or Made showcases the paths of those who have reached the upper echelons of business, revealing the secrets behind their success. Illuminated by powerful scriptures, these actionable strategies and expert insights from lifelong entrepreneur Larry Dix offer an inspiring roadmap to excellence. This is a book that is not just going to *tell* you how to get it done but will also *show* you exactly how to get it done! This is why I am excited about this book, and why I'm so supportive of Larry and all he is doing!

Again, if you are an entrepreneur, business leader, or individual looking to elevate your game, *Born or Made* is the book for you! You will be so glad you picked up this amazing book to help change your life for the better, which is what it has done for me. So, I hope you enjoy this great read and start implementing the action steps today to get your life where you want it to be!

Marques Ogden
Former NFL Athlete, CEO Ogden Ventures LLC

INTRODUCTION

"He told them another parable: 'The kingdom of heaven is like a mustard seed, which a man took and planted in his field. Though it is the smallest of all seeds, yet when it grows, it is the largest of garden plants and becomes a tree, so that the birds come and perch in its branches.'"
~ *Matthew 13:31-32 (NIV)* ~

As I sat down to write *Born or Made*, it wasn't just about telling my own story. It was about helping others walk the tough road of starting and running a business—a road I've traveled with no guide. I know how hard and lonely this journey can be. You're making big decisions, carrying the weight of your business, your family, and the people who depend on you. It's in these moments of solitude that your faith, your passion, and your purpose become your compass.

For much of my life, I faced challenges without leaning on scripture. I was just like anyone else, trying to find my way in the world, making mistakes, and learning the hard way. It wasn't until later that I began to understand the importance of faith, particularly in times of crisis. By writing this book, I realized how much scripture has guided me in ways I hadn't fully understood before. I want others to discover this guidance earlier than I did and use it to navigate the obstacles in their own journeys.

I've been through it all—the good times, the hard times, and those moments when I wondered if I was doing the right thing. Every challenge, every mistake, and every victory taught me something important. These lessons weren't meant just for me to keep; they're meant to be shared with others walking this same difficult road. And that's why I wrote *Born or Made*.

This book is for the night owls who stay up late planning, for the hard workers who get their hands dirty, and for the tough souls who keep getting back up after each fall. I'm sharing everything—the highs and the lows—that I wish someone had shared with me when I was starting out. This book isn't just words on a page; it's a friend walking beside you on your journey.

Throughout my journey, I've wrestled with the question: Are we born entrepreneurs, or are we made along the way? This question has shaped my path and the paths of so many others. So, I set out to answer it by speaking with hundreds of successful entrepreneurs. I wanted to know not just how they succeeded but how they faced their fears, dealt with failures, and found their true purpose.

The stories in this book offer insights not just into the challenges of business but also into the resilience of the human spirit and the power of faith. As you read through the pages, I want you to see yourself in the stories shared, learn from my journey, and feel encouraged in your own. You are not alone on this path, and no matter how tough it gets, if you stay faithful and focused, you'll find your way.

Just like the mustard seed, your purpose may start small, but with faith, passion, and perseverance, it will grow into something that can change your life—and the lives of others.

Chapter 1

THE ROAD TO GREATNESS

Embrace the Hustle, Flip Setbacks, and Build Grit

"Consider it pure joy, my brothers and sisters, whenever you face trials of many kinds, because you know that the testing of your faith produces perseverance. Let perseverance finish its work so that you may be mature and complete, not lacking anything."
~ James 1:2-4 (NIV) ~

From day one, I had this knack for hustling, a wild optimism, and dreams so big they could burst. But here's the thing that sets me apart: I'm all about taking the less-traveled road, seeing obstacles as chances to build grit, and turning every setback into rocket fuel for my passion. While others are kicking back on a Saturday night, you'll find me grinding away under the stars, laying the foundation for my dreams.

Just as the scripture above reminds us, every trial we face is an opportunity for growth. I've learned that setbacks aren't to be feared—they're opportunities to build resilience. The tougher the challenge, the stronger we become and the more we can achieve. Perseverance is the key to reaching new heights. Finding focus in the chaos of life has been my mission.

Weirdly enough, experiences like flying planes, which demand laser focus, and running marathons, which showed me how far I can push myself, have sharpened my ability to stay on target. Life is constantly changing us, and the real challenge is how we roll with those changes. My initial responses might not be flawless, but my determination to tackle challenges is rock-solid.

I've never struggled with admitting when I'm wrong—it's part of the deal, just like giving others a break when they mess up. Sure, I might not always be the sharpest tool in the shed, but my conviction is unbreakable. Push me, and I'll come back swinging with even more drive to prove you wrong. My wife, who doesn't dish out compliments easily, calls me the most passionate person she's ever met, and that means the world to me.

This journey is one big learning curve: I'm constantly soaking up new stuff. I've learned there's no shortcut to success. Every setback is a choice—be inspired or be defeated. I remember being called the "dumbest motherf****r" for not going to college. Those words didn't crush me; they fired me up to show that unconventional paths and resilience are worth their weight in gold.

I've always had this drive to achieve something big, even when I didn't fully get it back in the day. It's like an inner spark pushing me to do more. Setbacks don't keep me down for long; they just fuel my desire to get better. Failure has been my most fantastic teacher. Tough times are coming, no doubt, but each challenge is a chance to grow. I've learned to find the silver lining in most situations and turn defeats into motivation. This is all part of the journey to becoming the best version of ourselves.

Greatness isn't about what you're born with—it's about how you handle the rough patches along the way. The most complex tasks, the ones that push you out of your comfort zone, are the ones that build mental strength and resilience. So, don't rely solely on your natural talents. Embrace the struggle. It's through overcoming obstacles that you really achieve greatness.

If you're facing challenges, what is my advice? Dive in headfirst. There's a sea of self-help books and programs out there, but let's be honest—they're also businesses looking to cash in. Sure, they offer tips, but they're not magic fixes. We've made things way too complicated with all the info overload—from books to videos to social media noise. Don't fall for the hype. Some online resources are genuinely helpful, but you've got to sift through the nonsense to find them.

These traits aren't what we're born with—they're what we develop over time. I struggled with reading as a kid, but I didn't give up. By my mid-thirties, I tackled it head-on, making a habit of reading regularly. It wasn't about how many books I finished but what I learned from them. Reading opened new worlds and perspectives for me, and I'd encourage everyone to dive into it. Talent is great, but the real value comes from what we achieve through effort and persistence.

Looking back on my childhood, I'm struck by the freedom I had—no cell phones, no seat belts, just pure exploration and adventure. Nowadays, it feels like we're wrapping our kids in bubble wrap. It's the same in our workplaces, where just showing up on time is celebrated, no matter how well you perform. This trend worries me; at sixty, I fear seeing the country's decline. But I still believe in change. We all have the potential for greatness; it's about embracing challenges and striving to become our best selves. Entrepreneurship, often glamorized and oversimplified, is one of the toughest paths to take. But it's by facing our inner demons that we uncover our true potential. Each of us is unique and has the power to leave a lasting impact on the world. This belief drove me to write *Born or Made*, hoping it would inspire others on their entrepreneurial journey.

Setting bold goals has always driven me. I remember aiming to run a marathon, a dream that came true while building Apex. I not only ran one but completed two marathons within six months. I encourage everyone to set their own milestones and chase them with everything they've got. Time slips away, and childhood dreams can fade if we don't bring them to life. Whether it's learning to ski, taking a hot air balloon ride, skydiving, or hiking the Appalachian Trail, no goal is too small to pursue. Entrepreneurs often get lost in their ventures, but personal goals enrich our journey and reinforce our belief in what we can achieve. Some skills are innate, while others are developed through hard work and determination.

Learning to fly was a dream I pushed aside until a friend's terminal cancer diagnosis shook me into action. Watching his struggle made me realize how fragile life is and the need to chase our dreams while we can. I took on flight training and earned my pilot's license in six months. That achievement was a milestone in my life, and for the subsequent fourteen years, I enjoyed the freedom of the skies before selling my planes. This taught me the importance of seizing the moment and turning our dreams into reality, no matter the hurdles.

Throughout my journey, I've explored all kinds of businesses and picked up various skills, from vitamins and laundromats to real estate and truss manufacturing. I've delved into car dealerships, car washes, and more, all while keeping up with personal passions like writing, blogging, podcasting, and racing. This wide range of experiences reflects my commitment to growth and exploration in all areas of life.

In moments of reflection, I find comfort in knowing we're all a bit crazy in our own ways. Life constantly molds us, but deep down, we stay true to who we were from the start. Whether through gradual changes or sudden shifts, we evolve. Being a pallbearer has given me a deeper appreciation for life, reminding me to cherish every moment. It pains me when people are celebrated only after they're gone, fueling my drive to celebrate people while they're still here. We're born with certain traits, but life lets us adapt and refine them. Sometimes, change comes through hard work; other times, it's a blunt force. Despite the challenges, I keep pushing for personal growth, especially in mental strength. The "born" part is easy; it's the journey of becoming that truly tests us.

After devouring countless books, I've noticed they all tell a similar story: regular folks trying to be their best selves. I want to be a symbol of hope for anyone feeling defeated, letting them know they can keep going. Change doesn't happen overnight—I'm proof of that at 60. But through life's challenges and lessons, I believe both our nature and experiences shape us. As I write this book, I'm still working on becoming better myself. I hope each reader finds encouragement to keep improving, just like I am.

Exploring the Traits of the Top 1 Percent of Entrepreneurs

Alright, let's break it down. What sets the top 1 percent of entrepreneurs apart—not just those who rake in the cash, but the real trailblazers, the visionaries, the relentless doers? We're a unique breed, thriving on risk and unafraid to bet it all. Failure isn't just a chance; it's a constant companion. A staggering 97 percent of new businesses flop within the first decade. Yet, here I am, twenty-four years deep in the entrepreneurial game, still going strong. Stability is a foreign concept to us; we're the ones dancing on the edge of uncertainty.

"You strive for perfection, and you settle for excellence." ~ Joe Tomarchio

Let me guide you through the wild terrain of entrepreneurship. It's a journey full of pitfalls, where success is earned with relentless resolve and grit. To make it in this world, you need resilience as tough as old leather, impervious to the blows from naysayers and setbacks alike. You have to stand tall against adversity, weathering storms with unwavering determination to come out the other side intact.

> *"You know, most people just don't try, like I said, they talk,*
> *and they don't try and you have to kind of jump in.*
> *You can't wait for the perfect situation.*
> *It's never gonna be perfect. So you gotta just go for it."*
> ~ Max Gottlieb

But our grit isn't just tested by the outside world; it's our internal fortitude that really counts. The ability to face failure head-on, to see each setback as a stepping stone rather than a brick wall, is what defines a true entrepreneur. We're warriors of the mind, equipped with an unbreakable spirit that refuses to give up.

In this world of uncertainty, where success hangs by a thread, mental strength is our secret weapon. Navigating through doubt and uncertainty with unwavering resolve is what sets us apart from the crowd. We need to embrace challenges as chances to grow, seeing each setback as a lesson rather than a defeat.

Yet, for all our resilience and determination, we're not alone in this journey. While entrepreneurship might feel solitary, it's not without companionship. A shared sense of purpose unites us, a collective drive for greatness that goes beyond individual goals. In this camaraderie, we find strength, knowing we're part of a community that understands our struggles and celebrates our victories.

So, if you're stepping into the world of entrepreneurship or navigating its treacherous waters, remember this: it's not about having an innate talent or a smooth ride. It's about perseverance, resilience, and the relentless pursuit of your dreams. Embrace the challenges, learn from the failures, and keep pushing forward with grit and determination. In the end, it's your journey, your grit, and your unwavering spirit that will define your success.

What Drives Us

"Sports, racing, and entrepreneurs go hand in hand. Like every one of these guys I've run with, they own their own businesses and started something. Most of them, like yourself, had an idea that people probably thought was crazy. They went out and did it." ~ Kevin Conway

But what fuels this relentless pursuit of excellence? What compels us to brave the uncertainties of the entrepreneurial journey, defying the odds and carving our own paths to success? At its core, our drive stems from a deep-seated desire to leave a lasting legacy. We want to build something that transcends time and space, something that resonates long after we're gone. It's about purpose—this burning need to make our mark on the world.

Yet, it's not just the pursuit of glory that propels us; it's also the fear of failure. That fear is a powerful motivator, pushing us ever onward. Failure isn't just a setback; it's a crucible where our resolve is tested and tempered. It's through these failures that we learn, grow, and ultimately prevail.

When we encounter obstacles, retreat is not an option. Instead, we innovate. Challenges become opportunities for growth, invitations to push the limits of what's possible. It's this relentless pursuit of innovation that keeps us moving forward, propelling us closer to our goals.

> *"You have to be consistent, persistent, relentless, and redundant with perseverance. Each time, every time, all the time. To beat me, you have to eat me. If I haven't won, the war isn't over. Winners find a way, and losers find an excuse—or hire a lawyer to have one for them. Be a winner."* ~ Joe Tomarchio

Amidst the chaos and uncertainty of the entrepreneurial journey, one thing remains constant: our unwavering commitment to honesty and integrity. Without these guiding principles, success is just an illusion—a house of cards waiting to crumble at the slightest breeze.

In the end, we're not defined by our successes or failures but by our commitment to our ideals. We are dreamers, doers, and relentless pursuers of greatness. And while the path may be littered with obstacles, we press on, fueled by an unshakable belief in ourselves and our ability to change the world.

> *"So, I think the biggest thing that I've learned on this journey is authenticity to yourself, and being truthful with yourself, and even discovering what your own truth is. And that sounds kind of weird, but really dialing in on why you want to be successful."* ~ Kevin Conway

This authenticity is our compass, guiding us through the storm and ensuring we stay true to our vision. As we navigate the wild ride of entrepreneurship, let's embrace both our fears and our dreams, using them as fuel to drive us forward in our quest for greatness. One of the ways I fuel my fire is through interaction with others—especially positive people. When you surround yourself with those who are enthusiastic and share their stories, their energy can light a spark in you. Figures like Teddy Roosevelt and Elon Musk inspire me with their intelligence and innovative thinking. Simple dinners and quiet time with my wife recharge my batteries, while my grandchildren, with their youthful exuberance, bring immense joy and remind me of the wonder in life.

Hearing about others' successful journeys, including their trials and tribulations, invigorates me. It's a reminder that you're not alone as you navigate your journey. Many before you have faced similar struggles, and many will follow. The road is rarely straightforward, and I've learned that there are no shortcuts. You must be willing to tap into the energy and experiences of others to grow.

"The integrity of the upright guides them
but the unfaithful are destroyed by their duplicity."
~ Proverbs 11:3 (NIV) ~

Chapter 2

ORIGINS AND INFLUENCES

The Role of Upbringing in Entrepreneurial Success

*"Start children off on the way they should go,
and even when they are old they will not turn from it."*
~ Proverbs 22:6 (NIV) ~

Early experiences shape our trajectory, often in ways both positive and negative. I chose to use these experiences as motivation rather than defeat. My childhood was marked by a series of challenging situations that became pivotal moments in my growth. For instance, at age eight, I narrowly escaped a potential abuse situation, which instilled in me a resolve never to let such vulnerability occur again. I also faced physical confrontations and betrayal from peers, which fueled my determination to become stronger and more resilient.

Proverbs 22:6 reminds us that the foundation laid for us in our youth can shape the course of our lives. Just as our parents' guidance and early experiences influence our paths, it's clear that how we respond to our upbringing—whether positive or negative—has a profound impact on our entrepreneurial journey. By reflecting on the lessons learned from both struggles and support, we can harness that wisdom to fuel our drive and help shape our future successes.

These experiences, while painful, were instrumental in my personal development. I learned early on that it wasn't about avoiding challenges but about how I responded to them. I vowed never to be a follower or to be ridiculed without a fight. Even today, when faced with business setbacks, I find inspiration in observing others and using that as motivation to outperform them.

Reflecting on my upbringing, I realize how fortunate I was to have supportive parents. Both my parents were ferocious readers and very intelligent because they spent so much time reading. I never started reading until I was in my early thirties, and I think about how much I've learned from just the time spent reading. They set such great examples on so many fronts—not just in work ethic but in life in general. Thanks, Mom and Dad!

Being born in 1963 was obviously very different from today. Parental controls and safety measures were not as prevalent as they are now. I remember riding my bike back and forth to school, which seemed like miles but was probably not that far. In Corpus Christi, I would sometimes get lost exploring routes my parents had warned me against, but I always managed to find my way home safely. Reflecting on how different things were back then, I realize we didn't hear about dangers as frequently as we do now. For instance, we would poke rattlesnakes with mesquite tree branches and ride horses without saddles or bridles, simply using their manes to guide them. These experiences, though risky, were part of the learning process. Today, such activities might seem reckless, but they were formative for us. We never let fears hold us back, and somehow, we made it through without significant harm.

I can remember the first time I stuck a paperclip in an electrical outlet when I was eight years old. It shocked the crap out of me, and I can assure you I never did that again. The point of such an experience is that life's challenges create scar tissue that helps us learn and grow. Nowadays, it seems like we take all the risks out of everything, which can be a real challenge for entrepreneurs. We must be willing to take risks, break some bones, get them fixed, and get back to it. I can remember on two occasions as a kid getting concussions and not even going to the doctor. These experiences taught me resilience and the importance of learning from mistakes, which is crucial for entrepreneurial success.

I think about how hard it is for me to consider starting a business like Apex today at sixty years old because I'm so much more fearful and calculated. What a great time it was to start things when you're young and nonchalant about fear because you're really not aware of it. The entrepreneurial landscape is not necessarily more brutal today; it's just different. The abundance of information available now, compared to fifty or even thirty years ago when you had to go to a library or conduct extensive research, has changed the game. You can Google almost anything and find answers in minutes or turn to YouTube for tutorials. While this makes information more accessible, it also leads to information overload, which can be overwhelming.

Today, many people avoid uncomfortable situations, opting instead for emails and virtual communication rather than making cold calls or engaging in face-to-face interactions. To truly excel, you must become comfortable being uncomfortable until it becomes easy. They say public speaking is a common fear, but after doing it twenty or thirty times, it becomes second nature. The same principle applies to sales and other areas of business. You just need to persist through discomfort until you master it, and it feels natural.

One significant lesson I learned came from a turning point early in my career. About forty years ago, while working as a yard dog at a lumber company, I went out with friends on a Thursday night and got hammered. I rolled into work late, and as I was coming down from stacking lumber in the shed, the general manager, Dale Magoney, approached me. It was early in the morning, and I was extremely hungover. He greeted me with small talk before directly addressing my tardiness, saying, *"You were late this morning,"* to which I replied, *"Yes, sir, I was."* He then simply stated, *"That's never gonna happen again, is it?"* I responded, *"No, sir, it won't."* This brief but impactful conversation became a turning point for me. Dale's approach was not aggressive; it was clear and direct, and it made a strong impression. From that moment on, I was determined never to repeat that mistake. This lesson in accountability and self-discipline has stayed with me throughout my life, teaching me to use experiences, however challenging, as opportunities for growth.

For Those with Positive Parental Upbringing:

If you were fortunate to have a supportive and encouraging upbringing, you likely carry a sense of confidence and stability into your entrepreneurial endeavors. Use this positive foundation to fuel your ambitions. Reflect on the ways your parents' support has shaped your approach to challenges and opportunities. Embrace the confidence and resilience instilled in you to take bold steps and make impactful decisions. Ensure you continue to nurture your strengths while remaining humble and open to growth. Your positive upbringing provides a solid base, but the ongoing journey involves continual learning and adaptation.

For Those with Negative Parental Upbringing:

If your upbringing was marked by challenges or negativity, you might have developed a strong sense of self-reliance and resilience as a result. Recognize how these experiences have shaped your drive and determination. Use your past difficulties as a source of strength, fueling your desire to overcome obstacles and succeed. Seek out mentors and supportive networks to fill the gaps left by your early experiences. Embrace your ability to transform adversity into opportunity and continually reflect on how your background influences your decisions. While your past needn't define your future, understanding it can help you make meaningful adjustments on your path to success.

Whether your upbringing was positive or negative, it has likely had a significant impact on who you are today and the decisions you make. Reflect on your experiences: How have they shaped you? How have they influenced your choices and your approach to challenges? Consider what adjustments you might make now based on this reflection to help you move forward on your path to success. Embrace your past, learn from it, and use it as a foundation to build your future achievements.

The Power of Mentorship

Mentors are like a great book: if it's good, you'll want to read it again and again, and it'll leave a lasting impact on your life. If it's terrible, well, you won't even finish it. Looking back at my journey, I can honestly say I wouldn't be where I am today without the mentors who guided me. And let's be real— sometimes, the people around you can provide just as much guidance as a formal mentor. Even a single quote can stick with you for life and inspire you during tough times.

We often overlook the value of these relationships while we're caught up in the hustle. But when you look back, it's clear just how impactful they've been. Throughout my career, I had three pivotal figures who shaped my path. Each one was unique, yet all were incredibly smart and left their mark on me—some positively, some with harsh lessons. Those experiences, especially during economic struggles, helped mold me into the businessperson I am today.

As we grow older, it's essential to not only seek out mentors but also to step into that role ourselves. Remember, the guidance doesn't just flow in one direction. Just as I learned from others, it's our responsibility to pass knowledge down and help those who are coming up behind us. Great parents and grandparents can set the stage as your original mentors, providing the foundation you need to seek out additional wisdom as you navigate your journey. I was fortunate to have that kind of support, and it's made all the difference.

Mentors serve as guidance counselors through the chaotic life of business. Why wouldn't you seek those types of relationships? I've made plenty of mistakes along the way, and trust me, it's better to learn from someone else's missteps than to repeat them yourself. Mistakes are inevitable, but they can also be influential teachers that turn you into a great mentor in your own right.

Sometimes, I think people hesitate to help others because they fear being outshined or overshadowed. Not me. It brings me immense joy to see others succeed. In the end, there are no shortcuts in this game. Whether you're mentoring or being mentored, what you put in is what you get out. So, dig deep, invest in these relationships, and watch how they can transform your journey.

"Fathers, do not exasperate your children;
instead, bring them up in the training
and instruction of the Lord."
~ Ephesians 6:4 (NIV) ~

Chapter 3

THE ENTREPRENEURIAL MINDSET

Developing a Resilient Mind

"Do not be anxious about anything, but in every situation,
by prayer and petition, with thanksgiving, present your requests
to God. And the peace of God, which transcends all understanding,
will guard your hearts and your minds in Christ Jesus."
~ Philippians 4:6-7 (NIV) ~

Being resilient as an entrepreneur isn't just a skill—it's a requirement. You're stepping into a battlefield where most people will quit at the first sign of trouble, and you have to be prepared to stand tall, no matter what's coming at you. To thrive at the top of the food chain, you must embrace the mentality of the apex predator. As much as I value kindness—opening the door for my wife and kids, treating people with respect—don't mistake that for weakness. When the trumpet sounds, I'll be the first to respond. In business, you can't let fear or laziness take over. Too many men are letting the hyenas run their lives because they're afraid of what others might say. But remember, if God is with you, who can defeat you?

Philippians 4:6–7 reminds us to replace anxiety with prayer and trust in God's peace. In the entrepreneurial journey, uncertainties and challenges can be overwhelming. By turning to prayer and maintaining a thankful heart, we cultivate inner peace that strengthens our resilience. This divine peace guards our minds, enabling us to face business battles with calm and clarity.

Every challenge we face is an invitation to develop perseverance, which is essential for entrepreneurial success. As perseverance strengthens our resolve, it leads us toward maturity and greater success. Doing what's right is rarely easy, but it's always the right thing, no matter what people think. I'm not here to be your buddy—I'm here to make you the best version of yourself. When you succeed, you'll look back and realize that I was pushing you for your own good. We're not just raising cubs; we're shaping future lions. They might seem soft and sweet when they're young, but we need to prepare them for the real world—to grow into the apex predators they're meant to be, not stuffed animals off a Walmart shelf.

Developing a resilient mind is an ongoing process. Unlike physical fitness, which has visible results, mental strength requires internal work and self-awareness. Challenging yourself physically and mentally can help build resilience. Engaging in challenging tasks, learning continuously, and pushing beyond your perceived limits are essential for fostering mental toughness.

One significant experience in my entrepreneurial journey was in March 2010, when I faced a financial crisis that nearly led to bankruptcy. I remember meeting with a bankruptcy attorney who explained our situation and offered a path out—

filing for bankruptcy and starting fresh. However, the immediate hurdle was that I couldn't afford the $10,000 fee required to initiate the process. The attorney's response was blunt: *"Yeah, that could be a problem."* This stark realization led me to seek advice from local business experts, who bluntly told me that bankruptcy was inevitable.

Despite the discouraging news, I chose to double down on our efforts rather than give up. I decided that if we were going down, we would do so spectacularly. In the midst of this struggle, we brought our company credit card machine home to manage payroll and expenses. Using the credit card to cover gaps in cash flow was a short-term fix, and although it was a tough solution, it helped us keep going. Our accountant was astonished by our unconventional approach but ultimately recognized our determination. His words, *"If you can survive this, you're going to make a lot of money someday,"* proved prophetic.

Being resilient as an entrepreneur requires maintaining a positive outlook, even when facing significant obstacles. It involves believing in yourself when others might not and continuing to push through challenges that seem insurmountable. The entrepreneurial journey often involves extended periods of solitude and sacrifice, but it also offers the potential for great rewards.

One way I build resilience is through physical challenges, which help me develop mental toughness. Pushing past physical limits reinforces the understanding that when the mind tells you to stop, the body can often continue much further. This principle extends beyond physical endurance to the mental realm, where building resilience involves consistently challenging oneself and embracing discomfort.

Remember, the journey of entrepreneurship is full of ups and downs. Embrace the challenges, learn from failures, and keep pushing forward. The path may be lonely and filled with obstacles, but the rewards are worth the effort. Developing mental resilience is key to navigating this journey and achieving long-term success.

One of the ways I have developed mental resilience is through physical challenges. I believe that when your mind tells you to stop, you're only 40 percent of the way through your potential. The body is capable of far more than the mind often realizes. This principle extends beyond physical endurance to mental resilience. We are walking around with the most complex machine ever developed—our minds. I've spent a significant part of my adult life building the mental strength to endure the demands and beatings that come with running a business.

The mind can be your greatest enemy, capable of inflicting damage in ways that no external force can. I vividly remember my difficult times from 2008–2012, when stress and fear were overwhelming. I learned from a therapist that our perception of danger—like imagining a gun pointed at our head—affects our body as if the danger were real. This realization helped me understand the damage that stress and worry could inflict on my body. Developing mental strength is similar to building physical muscle; it requires pushing limits and enduring challenges.

Developing a resilient mind starts with the power of positive thinking. When I was a young man working at a lumberyard, during a challenging period for the company, I was moved back to the contractor's counter. One morning, I received a call to visit the Vice President's office. They asked if I could drive to San Antonio early the next day to pick up ceiling tiles for a new store we were building. I was asked to be there at 7:30 AM, which meant I would need to leave at 4:00 a.m.

Some people might have seen this request as a demeaning or menial task, perhaps feeling singled out or wondering why they were chosen for such an assignment. They might have thought it was beneath them or questioned why they had to do it when others could have done the job. Negative thoughts like, *"Why me?"* or *"This isn't my job"* might have arisen.

However, my perspective was different. Instead of feeling slighted, I felt a deep sense of pride and excitement. Out of the several hundred employees, I was chosen for this important task. It was an opportunity to prove my reliability and dedication. I saw it as a chance to contribute in a meaningful way, and I was grateful for the trust they placed in me.

Years later, I still look back on that experience with a positive mindset. It taught me that how we view a situation—whether as a challenge or an opportunity—depends mainly on our perspective. Maintaining a positive attitude is not just about being born with a sunny disposition; it's also about developing the ability to see the best in every situation. When you encounter tasks that seem trivial or inconvenient, remember that your attitude towards them can turn them into meaningful experiences. Embrace the chance to prove yourself and find pride in your contributions. The power of positive thinking can transform even the most mundane tasks into opportunities for growth and fulfillment.

Building resilience is essential in every aspect of entrepreneurship. You need to be willing to keep going when others quit, believe in yourself when no one else does, and understand that the prize is worth the effort, no matter how difficult the journey becomes. For me, one way I build resilience is through physical challenges. These tests push my body and mind to their limits and remind me that I'm capable of far more than I think. Every challenge I overcome adds to my mental strength, preparing me for the next big hurdle.

You've got to be ready to outwork, outmaneuver, and outlast everyone around you. Resilience means staying the course when the odds are against you, taking on challenges that others shy away from, and continuously building mental toughness to handle the beatdowns that life and business throw at you. That's the mindset of a true entrepreneur.

During the same period, I was offered a new role as an assistant manager at the south store. While retail was not my dream job, I was just grateful to have a position. Over time, I was entrusted with more responsibilities, like opening cash registers and balancing the vault on Saturdays. These tasks, which might have seemed small to others, exposed me to accounting functions and general ledger balancing that I wouldn't have learned otherwise. I was given the responsibility of handling tens of thousands of dollars, making bank deposits, and ensuring financial accuracy.

Many might have seen these responsibilities as beneath them, especially considering my previous role as the youngest outside salesman in the company's history. However, I embraced these opportunities with enthusiasm and gratitude. Being chosen for these tasks out of many others demonstrated their trust in me. I look back on these experiences with pride, knowing they contributed significantly to my growth and success. They taught me that even small opportunities can lead to significant advancements over time.

When I write about these experiences, I want entrepreneurs to know they are not alone in their struggles. If I can make the path a little easier for those coming behind me, it would bring me great joy. There are many of us out there grappling with the same challenges and striving for success. Embrace the journey and remember that resilience and determination can turn even the most challenging situations into opportunities for growth.

Navigating the entrepreneurial journey demands developing a resilient mind. Mental fortitude is crucial for handling challenges, overcoming obstacles, and staying motivated even when adversity strikes.

Fear Is a Liar

When I was on the verge of bankruptcy and overwhelmed by stress, my father advised me to seek help, leading me to a therapist whom I affectionately call the *"Green Witch."* During our first meeting, she noticed my stress and told me that bankruptcy would take ninety days if I decided to proceed, so I should relax. She explained that fears often concern things that might happen but don't happen immediately. She also taught me how my body reacts to perceived threats, even if they're not real, and guided me on deep breathing techniques to manage stress. She offered two options: take pills to feel better temporarily or take the hard route of reprogramming my mind. I chose the latter, knowing it was the only way to truly address the issue.

One critical lesson I learned is that fear often exaggerates problems, making them seem worse than they are. For example, waking up in the middle of the night with racing thoughts can amplify fears that are usually not as severe as they appear. Addressing fear involves recognizing it but not letting it control you. Fears are often exaggerated, and the body reacts to perceived threats as if they are real. This realization helped me manage stress and fear more effectively. Her advice on focusing on deep breathing and avoiding clock-watching during stressful times has been crucial in maintaining my mental well-being. Twelve years later, I'm still able to manage my stress effectively. One of her key pieces of advice was never to look at the clock when waking up in the middle of the night, a practice I still follow.

Fear can be a significant barrier to success. It distorts reality and creates unnecessary worry. I've learned to transform fear into motivation, using it as a driving force to confront challenges. The fear of failure was a powerful motivator, pushing me to persevere despite adversity. During the challenging years, the will to survive kept me going. Looking back, while it was a tough period, it wasn't as dire as it felt. I was broke, and many people in worse situations gave up. For me, quitting was never an option. Maybe it was naïve or even foolish, but I'm grateful I didn't give up. I can't imagine where I'd be today if I had thrown in the towel. I might have ended up working for someone else, constantly lamenting missed opportunities.

Fear is a thief, creating lies in our minds and distorting reality in powerful ways. I've learned to use fear as a motivator rather than letting it drag me down. Strengthening your mental resolve and pushing yourself to the limit can help transform fear into a driver for success. Failure is a fundamental ingredient in the recipe for success. To appreciate the wins, you must experience losses. Be prepared for many losses; you may face hundreds or even thousands before achieving a significant win. This is a core aspect of the entrepreneurial journey. Often, what you perceive as failures are merely minor setbacks.

The business world frequently overlooks the hours of pain and effort that go into training and mastering a trade. They only see the success, not the struggles. I often think of myself as a sixty-year-old overnight success, having started working at a young age. The pain and effort behind the scenes are seldom visible. Fear is one of the most enormous time and effort thieves because it can be debilitating. It's like having a pity party where only you are present.

We, as entrepreneurs, must accept that we are at the top of the food chain. We have responsibilities, not just to ourselves but to our families, our businesses, and our communities. Being at the top means we can't afford to let laziness or fear dictate our actions. I open doors for my family and show kindness—but make no mistake, kindness is not weakness. When it's time to act, when the trumpet sounds, I will be there. Too many men are letting the "hyenas" control their lives and businesses because they're scared of what others will think. But remember, doing what's right is rarely the most straightforward thing—but it's always the right thing.

I'm not here to be anyone's friend; I'm here to make you the best version of yourself that you can be. And one day, when you've made it, you'll realize that I was always on your side. We're raising cubs to become lions—strong, fierce, and independent. They won't become the lions they're meant to be by being coddled or treated like toys. We need to build them into the apex predators they are destined to be.

> "When I am afraid, I put my trust in you. In God,
> whose word I praise— in God I trust and am
> not afraid. What can mere mortals do to me?"
> ~ Psalm 56:3-4 (NIV) ~

Chapter 4

THE JOURNEY OF LEARNING

Acquiring Entrepreneurial Skills

"The beginning of wisdom is this: Get wisdom.
Though it cost all you have, get understanding."
~ Proverbs 4:7 (NIV) ~

Acquiring entrepreneurial skills is a challenge many face, and there's an ongoing debate about whether entrepreneurship is an innate ability or something that can be learned. It's true that some people seem to have a natural flair for it, while others may struggle to develop the necessary skills. However, the essence of entrepreneurship lies in the willingness to be uncomfortable. You must become comfortable with not knowing everything and, more importantly, not be afraid to ask the questions you need answers to.

In a way, Proverbs 4:7 reminds us that wisdom and understanding are essential on this journey—sometimes, it takes everything you've got to truly understand your path forward. Embrace the process of learning, whether from failure or success, and pursue wisdom relentlessly, for it is the foundation of growth and success in business.

One of the most valuable skills I've mastered over time is embracing the art of not knowing. I never shy away from admitting I don't have all the answers, but I'm always ready to find out. I've built a strong network of people I can reach out to—individuals who can help answer just about anything I need to know. Pride can be a significant barrier when it comes to learning. In a world as vast and complex as ours, you simply can't know everything, and that's okay. Surround yourself with people who know more than you; never be the smartest person in the room.

Another crucial aspect of acquiring entrepreneurial skills is the ability to embrace change. As a leader, you must accept that change is inevitable, even when those around you resist it. Leadership often means navigating through periods of discomfort, much like surviving a storm. When life throws challenges your way, you either adapt, learn, and move forward, or you let them defeat you. Complaining or resisting will get you nowhere, but learning from every situation will make you stronger.

Entrepreneurial skills extend beyond mere business tactics; they encompass integrity, overcoming defeat, finding the positive in adverse situations, and knowing when to say no. Success in business and in life often hinges on how well you learn from your mistakes and those of others. As Ray Dalio says, history repeats itself, and human behavior is predictable. By studying successful people, you'll find that they all experienced failures, but it was their ability to learn from those failures that ultimately led to their success.

Believing in yourself, even when doubt creeps in, is a skill in itself. It's about having the courage to trust your instincts, to see the bigger picture, and to take risks when necessary. Don't walk around with blinders on; there's a wealth of information all around you if you're paying attention. Observe the clues life offers—like a crowded movie theater, the number of new car tags you see, or trends in sales. If something doesn't make sense, trust that instinct.

I vividly remember the lead-up to the Great Recession. I saw it coming almost a year before most people, and that foresight saved me. Many people smarter than me didn't make it through, but I survived because I paid attention to the signs that others ignored. Don't overlook the small things; they often add up to something much larger.

Being an entrepreneur means accepting that this journey will be hard. It's not for the faint-hearted. If you're not willing to endure the hardships, it may be best to find a job that offers more security. But remember, most people who quit often look back with regret, wishing they hadn't given up. The entrepreneurial journey isn't easy, but for those who stick with it, the rewards—both personal and professional—are worth the effort.

The role of education in entrepreneurship has always intrigued me, especially given my unique experiences growing up. Watching my father graduate from college when I was just twelve years old, I often faced criticism for not following a traditional college path myself. It bothered me when people implied I was somehow less intelligent for not pursuing a degree. However, one key takeaway I've observed is that many graduates mistakenly believe their education ends once they receive their diploma. This is a significant error, particularly in today's world, where continuous learning is crucial.

As entrepreneurs, we must remain vigilant in educating ourselves about the economy's ever-changing landscape. I vividly recall 1986, a pivotal year when I entered my office only to find that half of my friends had been laid off. It was a stark wake-up call that propelled me to take control of my future. From that moment on, I committed to understanding how the stock market operates, the implications of interest rates, and the role of government monetary policy. This knowledge became vital for my survival and success.

If you're going to navigate the challenging journey of entrepreneurship, you need to grasp the broader economic picture. Too many people operate with a narrow focus, seeing only what's right in front of them. As entrepreneurs, we must adopt a panoramic view of our business environment, understanding the nuances better than anyone else. Ultimately, the only things you can truly control are your attitude, your effort, and your commitment to ongoing education. If you stop learning, you're effectively guaranteeing your struggle, if not outright failure.

I've learned that if you can endure tough times, a favorable economic climate will eventually come your way. In my case, it took twenty-two years before I experienced that turnaround. There were numerous downturns along the way, but persistence was key. It's essential to recognize that most businesses don't turn a profit in their first five years, and many fail in the next five. You must be prepared to do whatever it takes to survive and thrive, and education is your best ally.

Today, information is more accessible than ever. Back in my early days, I relied on newspapers, magazines, and limited television news, which often felt like watching propaganda designed to benefit someone else's agenda. By the time news broke, it was often too late for me to act. Now, with so much data at our fingertips, staying informed is easier than ever.

As entrepreneurs, we should not strive to be economists, but we must pay attention to the world around us. Observing consumer behavior—how many people are dining out, how many cars have new tags—can provide invaluable insights. Every interaction and observation contributes to our understanding of the market.

In essence, the entrepreneurial journey requires a commitment to continuous education and awareness. Don't be complacent; embrace every opportunity to learn and adapt. The information is out there, and it's up to you to seize it.

The School of Hard Knocks

Entrepreneurship isn't just about book smarts; it's also about learning from real-world experiences. Many successful entrepreneurs, including myself, didn't have the luxury of a formal education. Instead, we learned through trial and error, making mistakes and learning from them along the way.

One of the most valuable lessons I've learned is the importance of time management. In the early days of my business, I attended a class on using day planners, which taught me how to manage my time effectively. While day planners can still be helpful, modern technology offers even better tools. Today, there are numerous calendar and planning apps available that can help streamline your scheduling and task management. Apps like Trello, Asana, or Google Calendar allow you to organize your tasks, set reminders, and facilitate real-time collaboration with your team. These tools not only enhance efficiency but also ensure you stay on top of deadlines and priorities, freeing up mental space for creativity and strategy.

Another crucial lesson was the importance of documentation. By keeping meticulous records and having a "cover your ass" (CYA) box, I was able to resolve disputes and build trust with customers. This attention to detail and commitment to excellence set me apart from my competitors and helped me succeed in business. In the digital age, this can be easily accomplished with cloud storage solutions like Google Drive or Dropbox, where you can organize important documents, contracts, and communications in one accessible location.

Ultimately, the key to success in entrepreneurship is a combination of education, experience, and a willingness to learn and adapt. By continuously honing your skills and embracing new challenges, you can navigate the ups and downs of entrepreneurship and achieve your goals. Remember, success isn't just about reaching the top; it's about the journey and the lessons learned along the way. Embrace every opportunity to learn, whether it's from your own experiences or through the wealth of resources available at your fingertips.

"Ask and it will be given to you; seek and you will find; knock and the door will be opened to you."
~ Matthew 7:7 (NIV) ~

Chapter 5

PASSION AND PURPOSE

The Fuel for Entrepreneurial Fire

"You are the light of the world.
A town built on a hill cannot be hidden."
~ Matthew 5:14 (NIV) ~

Finding your purpose in life can often feel like searching for a needle in a haystack. But here's the good news: One of the most effective ways to discover your purpose is by looking closely at your passions. When you align what you love with what you do, that's where the magic happens. Passion fuels purpose, and when you ignite that fire, you can transform your life in extraordinary ways.

Much like the light that shines from a city on a hill, when you align your passion with your purpose, you can't help but stand out. Your energy and enthusiasm for what you do become visible to others, helping you grow, inspire, and create impact. Passion is the spark that lights the way for your entrepreneurial journey and gives you the power to persist, even through tough times.

First, let's take a moment to explore what passion really means. It's the driving force that makes you lose track of time, the activity that brings you joy and fulfillment. For some, it might be creating art; for others, it's solving complex problems, while for many, it's helping others achieve their dreams. Passion can take many forms, and it's deeply personal.

Think back to the moments in your life when you felt truly alive. Was it when you were on stage performing, in the kitchen whipping up a new recipe, or hiking up a mountain, feeling the wind in your hair? Those experiences are not just hobbies; they are windows into your soul. They reveal the things that make your heart race and your spirit soar.

Connecting Passion to Purpose

Now, how do we take those passions and transform them into a sense of purpose? The first step is reflection. Take some time to really think about what excites you. Write down a list of activities that make you feel energized and fulfilled. Next to each item, jot down how it impacts your life and the lives of others. This exercise can help you identify patterns and themes that can guide you toward your purpose.

Once you've got your list, it's time to dig deeper. Ask yourself questions like: What problems do I enjoy solving? How can I use my passions to make a difference? Who do I admire, and what do they do that resonates with me? These inquiries will help you connect your passions to a greater cause, a purpose that transcends yourself.

Finding your purpose is rarely a linear path; it often requires a willingness to explore and experiment. This is where the magic of trying new things comes into play. Don't be afraid to step outside your comfort zone. Attend workshops, take up new hobbies, volunteer for causes you care about, or even start small projects that align with your passions.

For example, if you love writing, try starting a blog or contributing articles to local publications. If you're passionate about cooking, consider hosting community cooking classes or starting a food-related business. These experiments can help you gain clarity on what truly resonates with you and what doesn't.

Another key aspect of discovering your purpose is the people you surround yourself with. Engage with others who share your passions or who inspire you in different ways. Attend networking events, join clubs, or participate in online forums related to your interests. When you immerse yourself in a community of like-minded individuals, you can exchange ideas, learn from each other's experiences, and gain valuable insights that can illuminate your path.

I recall a time when I joined a local entrepreneur group. Initially, I was nervous, thinking I didn't have much to offer. But as I listened to others share their stories, I realized that my own experiences and passions were worth sharing. The more I engaged with the group, the more I discovered how my passions could align with my purpose of helping others succeed.

Once you have a clearer sense of your passions and how they connect to your purpose, it's time to set intentions and goals. Intentions are the driving force behind your actions; they give you a sense of direction. Start by setting specific, measurable, achievable, relevant, and time-bound (SMART) goals that align with your newfound purpose.

For example, if you've discovered that your passion lies in helping others, your goal might be to volunteer at a local nonprofit for a certain number of hours each month or to start a community initiative. Break these goals down into smaller, manageable steps, and celebrate your progress along the way.

Remember that finding your purpose is a journey, not a destination. It may evolve over time, and that's perfectly okay. As you grow and change, your passions may shift, leading you to new purposes. Embrace the twists and turns, and don't be afraid to adjust your course as needed.

One of the most empowering aspects of this journey is that you can continuously revisit your passions and reassess how they align with your purpose. Life is dynamic, and so is your path. Keep your heart open and be willing to adapt.

Lastly, recognize that when you pursue your passions and live with purpose, you create a ripple effect. Your energy and enthusiasm can inspire those around you, encouraging them to pursue their own passions and find their purposes. As you ignite your fire, you also help others light theirs.

Passion and Purpose in Entrepreneurship

Entrepreneurship thrives on passion and purpose. Without these elements, the journey can feel empty, and achieving success becomes more challenging. Aligning your business with your passion is not just optional; it's essential. Passion fuels your determination when times get tough, while purpose keeps you focused on your long-term goals. Together, they form the foundation for entrepreneurial success.

Passion often finds you rather than the other way around. For me, it has never been about chasing money; money is simply a tool. The real motivation comes from deeper sources— whether it's proving others wrong, proving myself right, or achieving something once thought impossible. My wife often tells me I am the most passionate person she's ever met. My in-laws have expressed their confidence in me, knowing I will always take care of my wife, Sheryl, and our kids. This unwavering passion drives me forward.

Think of passion as a process similar to building a fence. You start at point A, aiming for point B, but along the way, you encounter rocks and obstacles. You may need to get a bigger auger or move the fence over a bit to keep building. Eventually, when you look back, you see a well-constructed fence, and the challenges you faced become mere memories. A year from now, you likely won't even think about those struggles. Instead, you'll recognize that the obstacles strengthened your resolve.

Every entrepreneurial journey must have a purpose. You will encounter incredibly difficult days, but if it were easy, everyone would be doing it. Your *purpose* is what sustains you through tough times. Currently, my motivation is to care for my wife in our later years, ensuring she has no financial worries. Additionally, I want to protect my grandchildren from the uncertainties of today's society and government. It's crucial to find your "why," understanding that it will evolve as you grow more successful. What motivates you now will shift over time.

Setting goals is essential—start with simple ones and build on your successes. Success is contagious, whether it's learning a new language, reading a set number of books, or running a marathon. If it motivates you, it's not foolish; pursue it wholeheartedly.

There was a time when someone called me the "dumbest motherf***er" for not going to college. That comment stuck with me for forty years, but in hindsight, I wish I could thank that person. His words fueled my drive. The guys who laughed at me while driving away inspired me to lift weights and become the best athlete I could be. Growing up with the last name "Dix" brought its own challenges, but I later realized that people will always find something to tease you about. What once bothered me no longer holds power over me; it only made me stronger.

My father had a difficult childhood but became incredibly successful. When I asked him how he did it, his answer was simple: *"I never looked back."* That's a valuable lesson for all of us. Life will throw challenges your way, and sometimes you'll get knocked down—maybe even break a bone. But those broken bones heal, and you must keep pushing forward. Always look for the silver lining in every setback.

If you genuinely want to be successful, learn to find the stars in the storm. No matter how dark it gets, the sun will rise again tomorrow. You have to keep moving forward, even when it feels impossible. Passion and purpose will guide you, but persistence is the key that unlocks long-term success.

In the end, don't let obstacles define you. Whether someone said you weren't smart enough or life threw unexpected hardships in your path, don't let it stop you. Use those experiences as fuel to propel you forward, to build something even stronger. Remember, the hardest challenges often lead to the greatest victories.

Finding your passion and purpose is essential to fueling your entrepreneurial journey. It's not just about the money or accolades; it's about the pride in knowing you overcame every obstacle and turned every doubter into a motivator. Keep building that fence. The rocks along the way are just part of what makes the final structure stronger.

For me, passion has always revolved around business and entrepreneurship. It has been in my blood since I was fifteen years old. While I didn't always know what kind of business I wanted to own, I knew I wanted to create something of my own. I never had a specific direction—my goal was always broader: simply to own a business. Looking back, this openness turned out to be a great advantage. I was willing to pivot and explore different paths while keeping my main objective in sight.

If you had told me at twenty years old that I would own a truss manufacturing facility, I would have first asked what a truss was. That's the beauty of being open to different opportunities—sometimes you end up somewhere completely unexpected, but it's exactly where you're meant to be. Don't get bogged down thinking there's only one path to your goals. Be willing to pivot and embrace opportunities as they arise; they might lead you precisely where you need to go.

The fun lies in building a business. Yes, I've been motivated by money, but it's never been the sole focus. Money is a tool—a means to achieve goals—but it doesn't define me or my success. The real reward comes from the results of my hard work—the satisfaction of knowing I've built something meaningful and made smart decisions along the way.

I find immense joy in using the money I've earned to help others. One of my greatest pleasures is giving without seeking recognition. It's fulfilling to contribute to others' lives while remaining anonymous.

So, when it comes to aligning your business with your passion and purpose, remember it's not just about the money. It's about doing what you love, building something meaningful, and using the results of your hard work to make an impact—

whether for yourself, your family, or others. That's what defines success for me: being an entrepreneur before it was cool, driven by a passion for business, and finding fulfillment in both the journey and the outcome.

For me, the driving purpose has always been to earn more money, viewing it as a tool to secure a better future for my family. As I've grown older, that focus hasn't shifted much, but my motivation has evolved. Now, at sixty, I'm working harder than ever, not just for myself but to ensure a brighter future for my grandchildren. I believe their future is at risk, and I want them to read this book someday and understand that their grandfather was not just driven by money; he was a highly motivated man willing to do whatever it took, within the law, to protect his family.

Unfortunately, this dedication has sometimes meant sacrificing time with my own children. However, I feel fortunate to have the chance to do things differently with my grandchildren. I refuse to let others dictate my thoughts or actions. I will stand firm and speak my mind, especially when it comes to my grandchildren's rights. With six granddaughters and two grandsons, I will do whatever it takes to give them a fighting chance—providing them with a good education and the freedom to make their own choices.

Seeing the innocence in small children and knowing how the world can sometimes work against them motivates me deeply. It baffles me how common sense often seems to be disregarded. I don't mind what others choose to do as long as they leave my family alone and allow us to live our lives freely.

As I write this book about the journey of an entrepreneur, I want to emphasize that there are no shortcuts in business or in life. Hard work is essential; the harder you work, the luckier you get. I want my children and grandchildren to remember this. When you're focused on your goals, you don't have time for trouble. You're too busy working hard and, ultimately, resting well at the end of the day. That's the legacy I aim to instill in them: the value of hard work and the importance of protecting what truly matters.

"Never be lacking in zeal, but keep your spiritual fervor, serving the Lord."
~ Romans 12:11 (NIV) ~

Chapter 6

SALES SALES SALES

"Do you not know that in a race all the runners run, but only one gets the prize? Run in such a way as to get the prize."
~ 1 Corinthians 9:24 (NIV) ~

In the context of sales, **1 Corinthians 9:24** reminds us that achieving success requires dedication, focus, and relentless effort. Just like in a race, every salesperson is competing, but only those who commit to going above and beyond, pushing through challenges, and staying disciplined will ultimately secure the prize—whether that's closing the deal, building lasting relationships, or driving business growth.

I may not always be the sharpest tool in the shed, but when it comes to selling, that's where I truly shine. It's not just about having the gift of gab; it's about instilling belief in what you're conveying. Trust me, that's a skill you won't find in any textbook.

To me, selling is an art form. It's about forging genuine connections with people, understanding their needs, and demonstrating how your offering aligns with those needs. Confidence plays a role, but sincerity is equally important. You have to genuinely believe in what you're selling, or no one else will.

Here's the kicker: You don't need to be the smartest person in the room to excel at sales. You have to be the most persuasive and the most passionate. Make people feel your conviction. When I engage with a customer, I'm not just pitching a product or service; I'm offering a solution to their problem. I'm helping them with my product. I guide them to see how what I offer can enhance their lives or businesses.

It all comes down to communication—clear, direct, and succinct. You need to grasp what the other person seeks and then convincingly illustrate how you can fulfill their need. When you hit that sweet spot, and you see the glint in their eyes that says, *"Yes, this guy gets it,"* then you know you've hit the bullseye.

I may not win a trivia contest, but when it comes to selling and making people believe in what I bring to the table, that's where I stand out. Exceptional salesmanship isn't about being the brightest; it's about being the most effective communicator—the one who can turn a *maybe* into a resounding *yes*.

Sales, in my book, is one of the most thrilling aspects of business. I often say, "Gotta make the cash register ring," because, without sales, nothing in business moves forward. Everything hinges on securing those sales first. This principle has always motivated me.

But let's be clear: When I talk about sales, I mean selling at a profit. Anyone can sell at a loss. Early on in my entrepreneurial journey, I learned this the hard way. I achieved significant sales figures but wasn't making the profit I should have. That's when I realized the importance of tightening operations, implementing procedures, and focusing on margins. As they say, margins matter—gross margin dollars are crucial. I could sell products cheaply all day long, but that wouldn't translate into profits.

So, as you navigate your sales journey, remember it's not just about the numbers. It's about connection, conviction, and the ability to communicate effectively. Embrace the challenges, learn from your experiences, and keep pushing forward. After all, in the world of business, every sale is a step toward your more remarkable legacy.

Sales are incredibly important, but margins are often overlooked. Margins represent the difference between sales revenue and the costs associated with producing and selling a product or service. They are crucial because they determine the profitability of your business. High margins allow for more flexibility in managing expenses and navigating economic downturns, while low margins can quickly lead to financial strain. Understanding and improving your margins is essential for sustainable growth and long-term success, as they directly influence your ability to reinvest in your business, pay your employees, and ultimately achieve your financial goals.

Let's break down why understanding margins can make or break your business, highlighting the risks of having high sales paired with low margins.

Consider two scenarios:

- $5,000,000 in sales at 40 percent margins results in $2,000,000 in gross margin dollars.
- $6,000,000 in sales at 30 percent margins yields only $1,800,000 in gross margin dollars.

At first glance, you might think the difference is just $200,000. However, higher sales often come with greater expenses—larger receivables, increased inventory, and potentially higher loans to support purchasing and maintaining stock. You might also face additional costs, like hiring more employees or increased shipping expenses. These factors can quickly turn a net profit into a break-even point or a loss.

I learned this lesson early in my entrepreneurial journey. In my third year, I sold $5.5 million but barely made any money. The following year, I reduced my sales by $1 million and turned a profit. How? I became more nimble, reducing the risk of unpaid receivables and lowering overhead. Before, I was fixated on selling, selling, selling. Then it hit me—I needed to start making money, and it was getting ridiculous to think otherwise.

Don't make the same mistake. Understand your costs. It's not just important to know them when times are good; it's crucial during harsh economic conditions. If you're selling something for $1.30, you better ensure you're making at least $0.30—because that small margin can be the difference between keeping the lights on and going out of business.

While sales drive activity and generate work, margins are equally, if not more, important. This aspect often doesn't get enough emphasis. Let's be honest: Anyone can give something away. The focus should be on creating value and driving margins. Sure, people might resist paying 10 or 20 percent more, but just a 1 or 2 percent increase can significantly impact your bottom line. Remember, we're all in this for profit—that's what gets us out of bed in the morning.

To meet your margins, it's essential to regularly analyze your costs and pricing strategies, ensuring that your sales prices reflect the value you provide while covering your expenses. If you find you're not meeting your margins initially, consider reevaluating your supply chain, reducing overhead costs, or adjusting your pricing to better align with the market. It's important to take a proactive approach, continuously monitoring your financials and making necessary adjustments. Remember, achieving margins is often a gradual process, and with persistence and strategic planning, you can turn initial setbacks into opportunities for improvement.

Know Your Product

I've always had a knack for sales. Give me a product, and I can sell it—provided I understand it inside and out. This skill was honed early on while studying product labels on the retail floor, where I learned that while you can bluster through with empty talk, true knowledge and understanding command respect and drive sales. Staying competitive is crucial, but I've discovered that customers are often willing to pay a bit more for quality and expertise.

When I say you need to know your product, I mean you have to REALLY dive deep—really deep. This isn't just about memorizing features; it's about understanding every nuance, from how it works to what sets it apart from competitors. Think of yourself as the Sherlock Holmes of your product; you should be able to answer any question thrown your way. When you engage with customers, they should feel like they're getting insider knowledge from an expert, and that expert should be you.

Early in my career, I learned this lesson on the retail floor at nineteen years old. A seasoned colleague advised me to read labels and understand the products when I had downtime. I took that advice seriously, and it transformed my approach. Suddenly, I was a young kid confidently explaining paint types to a much older customer, who was surprised to find out I knew more than he did. That connection built trust, and soon, customers were seeking me out regularly. My sales numbers climbed because I became a go-to resource.

Today, accessing product knowledge is even easier. The Internet offers a wealth of information at your fingertips. If you're not an expert on your product, the only reason is that you're not putting in the effort. Platforms like YouTube are invaluable; you can now learn about your product in minutes through videos that break down complex information. Gone are the days of poring over lengthy manuals. If you want to excel in sales, it's simple: Commit to learning everything you can about your product. Your dedication will set you apart and help you become a rock star in your field.

I remember my very first sales call at just twenty-one years old. Armed with a list of lumber to quote, I walked into the office of a seasoned customer, feeling confident. However, when I presented my quote, he quickly pointed out that my prices were high for treated materials and cedar. I stumbled, was caught off guard, and left feeling deflated.

Back at the office, I shared my experience with our sales manager. He asked me what I had communicated about our cedar. It hit me—I hadn't mentioned that our cedar is kiln-dried, not partially dried, which prevents shrinkage and justifies the premium. Similarly, our treated material was treated to a .40 ground contact level, compared to the .25 that others offered, which would eventually fail if directly in contact with the ground. Additionally, our plate material was utility grade, providing better quality with fewer knots than the number three grade.

This experience taught me the importance of understanding your product in relation to the competition. When you can effectively counter objections with solid information, you gain a significant advantage. I dedicated considerable time to learning about materials and their manufacturing processes, enabling me to respond confidently to any rebuttals. This valuable lesson learned at the age of twenty-one reinforced that knowledge is your strongest ally in sales.

Customer Service

Service, coupled with value, is the backbone of any successful business. I've always viewed our company not just as a manufacturer of roof and floor trusses but as a customer service-centric entity. Providing unparalleled customer service has been my mantra from day one. However, this doesn't mean the customer is always right. There are times when you need to assert yourself and say no.

I've observed a significant shortage of urgency and dedication in sales. When it comes to sales, being aggressively proactive with immediate callbacks and staying hyper-focused on solving problems can make all the difference. This approach not only helps customers perform their jobs more effectively but also builds lasting trust. Central to this strategy is a hyper-study of your product.

We've all heard the saying, *"The customer is always right,"* and in many cases, it holds true. For instance, the customer is unequivocally correct if I send out a load of trusses and they encounter issues with dimensions, overhangs, or possibly broken trusses. We have a policy to promptly address and fix these issues because maintaining trust is paramount. Another example is when a customer questions the cost of trusses for a high-pitch house. By analyzing their specific needs, such as reducing the truss height to save on transportation costs without compromising quality, we provide solutions that save them money and enhance their project efficiency.

Additionally, when a customer expresses concerns about delivery timelines impacting their project schedule, we prioritize expedited shipping and adjust our production schedules to meet their deadlines. By doing so, we demonstrate our commitment to their success, reinforcing that their needs are our top priority.

Of course, there are instances when the customer is wrong, and knowing when to stand firm is crucial. For example, if a customer approves a design and later claims it wasn't what they wanted, we must uphold the agreement since they signed off on the design. Another situation arises when a customer insists on using inferior materials to cut costs, jeopardizing the project's integrity. In such cases, we must educate them on the long-term benefits and cost savings of using higher-quality materials, even if it means walking away from the deal.

Furthermore, when a customer requests customization that falls outside our production capabilities, it's essential to explain our limitations clearly and offer alternative solutions that align with their needs without compromising our standards. This balance between flexibility and maintaining quality ensures we protect our reputation while striving to meet customer expectations.

Each case must be evaluated on its own merit, considering both immediate and long-term impacts. While it's important to avoid litigation at all costs, sometimes taking a stand is necessary to uphold our values and quality standards. My approach is always to seek a resolution that benefits both parties, fostering a relationship built on mutual respect and understanding.

Prioritizing exceptional customer service pays dividends and sets smaller players apart from corporate giants. However, this journey hasn't been a walk in the park. In the initial years, I couldn't afford to give trusses away. Rejection after rejection, seeing my business card tossed in the trash before I'd even left an office, was gut-wrenching. But I persevered because I knew persistence would pay off.

One memorable moment was when a long-time customer faced unexpected delays from their supplier. Instead of pointing fingers, we stepped in to expedite their order, ensuring their project stayed on track. Another time, a client was dissatisfied with the color finish on their trusses. We took immediate action to replace the affected pieces at no extra cost, turning their frustration into satisfaction.

Through these experiences, I've learned that understanding your product compared to your competitors is a huge advantage. When you can effectively counter objections with solid information, you gain a significant edge. I dedicated considerable time to learning about materials and their manufacturing processes, enabling me to respond confidently to any rebuttals. This valuable lesson learned at the age of twenty-one reinforced that knowledge is your strongest ally in sales.

Balancing exceptional customer service with product knowledge and strategic decision-making is the key to building a successful business. By knowing when to support the customer and when to stand firm, you create a foundation of trust and respect that drives long-term success. Whether it's reducing costs, addressing quality concerns, or navigating challenging situations, prioritizing service and value will set you apart and ensure your business thrives. Remember, customer service is still king. I may build roofs and floor trusses, but at the end of the day, I'm in the customer service business.

Finding Ways to Create Rapport

Sales, you see, is much like the real estate mantra: location, location, location. Securing a prime spot in your customers' minds is paramount. The goal is to create a mental association so strong that they think of you first when they need your product or service. But how do you achieve this?

Understanding Your Customer: When you walk into any corporate office, it's easy to gauge their priorities just by looking around. Take a moment to scan the walls for awards or historical articles displayed in the lobby. These pieces can provide valuable insights. For example, if you spot a newspaper article mentioning the company's founding in 1983, you can confidently say, *"I didn't know you started your business in 1983—congratulations!"* Starting off with a compliment not only shows that you've done your homework but also establishes a connection. Additionally, most companies showcase their achievements and plans on their websites, which can offer a wealth of information before you even set foot in the office. People appreciate recognition of their successes, so highlighting these in conversation can foster goodwill.

On a more personal note, an office can reveal a lot about the individual. From family photos to sports memorabilia, these items provide clues about their interests and values. You can absorb a wealth of information without saying a word, making it easier to build rapport and establish a genuine connection during your visit. The first step is to establish a genuine connection. Look for every angle to relate to your customer. Empathy is key. Look around their store and office and observe. Take the time to learn about their interests, hobbies, and family. Are there pictures on the wall that give you clues? Perhaps they have a family photo or a framed duck hunting picture. Use these as conversation starters to create rapport.

1. **Engaging in Conversation:** If you notice a picture of their child who just graduated from college, share a similar experience about your own child. This common ground makes you relatable and memorable. It's not just about selling; it's about building a human connection.

2. **Observing Details:** Pay attention to details if you're not in their office. Does the person wear a distinctive watch? Are they dressed in golf attire? Do they drive a car you can relate to? These small cues can open doors to conversations about shared interests. If you both enjoy golfing, for example, ask about their favorite courses or recent outings. This shows you care about them as a person, not just as a customer.

3. **Building a Narrative:** As you create these connections, weave them into a narrative. For instance, if you both

have kids and you've been through similar experiences, share those stories. This not only strengthens your bond but also makes you memorable. When they think of their needs, they'll remember the person who shared their story.

4. **Finding Common Ground:** Look for shared experiences or interests, such as favorite hobbies, sports teams, or local events. This can help you create a comfortable atmosphere. For example, if you discover that you both support the same sports team, you can use that as a touchpoint to break the ice.

5. **Active Listening:** During your conversation, practice active listening. Show genuine interest in what they're saying by nodding, maintaining eye contact, and asking follow-up questions. This demonstrates you value their thoughts and opinions, further solidifying your connection.

6. **Using Humor:** If appropriate, light humor can break down barriers and make the interaction more enjoyable. A well-timed joke or a light-hearted comment can create a relaxed atmosphere, making it easier for both of you to connect.

7. **Following Up:** After the initial meeting, follow up with a personalized message that references your conversation. If you talked about a family trip they were planning, send a quick note wishing them well. This reinforces the connection and keeps you at the top of their mind.

By taking these steps, you knock down barriers and become a relatable human being rather than just another salesperson trying to make a quick buck. Many people view salespeople with skepticism, assuming they're just after a commission. By building authentic connections, you position yourself as a trusted partner who genuinely cares about their needs.

Sales is about more than just transactions; it's about relationships. When you create these mental associations, you're not just securing a sale—you're fostering loyalty that can last for years to come. And that, in the world of sales, is the ultimate goal.

But here's the kicker—sales isn't just about pushing products; it's about creating value. A fundamental aspect of this is respecting not only your own time but also your customers' time. When you demonstrate that you value their time as much as your own, you send a powerful message: you care about their needs and priorities. This approach fosters an environment of mutual respect and understanding, which is vital in building strong relationships.

Stop trying to compete on price alone—that's a race to the bottom. Instead, focus on demonstrating the true value of what you're offering. Whether it saves time, enhances efficiency, or simplifies their lives, make sure your customers recognize these benefits. When people see how your product can positively impact their lives, they'll be eager to invest, regardless of the price. Highlighting the real value not only sets you apart from competitors but also builds lasting relationships based on trust and satisfaction. So, communicate effectively, and watch as customers line up for what you bring to the table.

One way I embody this principle is by always aiming to under-commit and over-perform. It's a straightforward strategy: promise less than what you can deliver and then exceed those expectations. For instance, if you estimate that a project will take two weeks, aim to complete it in ten days. Not only does this approach showcase your reliability, but it also leaves your customers pleasantly surprised. This creates a positive impression that they will remember, reinforcing the idea that you are someone they can count on.

Trust, my friend, is the cornerstone of any lasting relationship, whether in sales or any other aspect of life. When customers see that you consistently deliver on your promises, they are more likely to return to you in the future. They begin to view you as a trusted advisor rather than just a salesperson. This shift in perception is crucial because it opens the door to deeper conversations about their needs, enabling you to provide even more tailored solutions.

Furthermore, cultivating trust leads to referrals and recommendations. Satisfied customers are likely to share their positive experiences with others, creating a ripple effect that can significantly expand your client base. In a world where competition is fierce, having a solid reputation built on trust can set you apart. It's not just about making a sale; it's about fostering relationships that create ongoing value for both you and your customers.

In the end, sales are not merely transactional; they're relational. Respecting your customers' time by under-promising and over-delivering cultivates trust and loyalty. These elements are the true drivers of long-term success in sales and are essential for creating a sustainable business. So, the next time you interact with a customer, remember that your approach can turn a simple transaction into a lasting partnership.

> *"I noticed when I walk into a room, right, have a conversation with somebody, if I'm really passionate about something, and I believe in it, I can sell it."*
> ~ Max Gottlieb, Hollywood Producer, and Talent Manager.

Empathy

Now, let's talk about empathy—a quality often overlooked in sales. Empathy allows you to connect with people on a deeper level, regardless of their position. It's not about preconceived notions based on titles; it's about treating everyone with respect. Dick Marriott once mentioned that his greatest success in business stemmed from his ability to empathize with individuals at all levels, and that struck a chord with me. I've always prided myself on my ability to converse with anyone, from the janitor to the CEO, without bias. In sales, every interaction matters, and everyone plays a role.

So, how can you cultivate empathy in your interactions? While some people find it comes naturally, there are simple ways to develop this vital skill. First, remember that everyone shares everyday experiences. We all have our challenges—whether dealing with a frustrating spouse, managing a busy schedule, or facing everyday annoyances. By acknowledging that everyone has their struggles, you create a connection.

One of the easiest ways to practice empathy is to engage with others genuinely. Reflect on your experiences and use what you learned from them to forge and deepen connections. Having worked my way up from yard dog to CEO, I truly understand what it feels like to be looked down upon. This background fuels my desire to treat everyone with respect. After all, in sales, we rely on the contributions of many people. Being nice to everyone is essential because, as the saying goes, *"You catch more flies with honey."*

Think about it: When you're at the grocery store, and the cashier is checking you out, you should be nice to them. They have a demanding job and deal with difficult customers all day long. Be the person they remember tonight because you were kind, not the jerk who added to their stress.

Always remember that everyone has their own life and challenges. By being kind and approachable, you not only create a positive atmosphere but also build meaningful connections that can enhance your sales career. Empathy may not always come easy, but making a conscious effort to connect with others will pay off in your personal and professional life.

Honesty

In manufacturing, honesty is non-negotiable. You're constantly juggling capacity and deadlines; it's like walking a tightrope—one misstep, and you're in for a tumble. That's why I've always believed in transparency. If a delivery is delayed, I'd rather under-promise and over-deliver than leave a customer hanging. Being upfront about potential setbacks not only builds trust but also sets realistic expectations.

Transparency can manifest in various ways across different industries. For instance, in the tech sector, software companies often face the challenge of managing updates and bug fixes. If a release is delayed, they can keep their users informed through regular updates, explaining the reasons for the delay and the steps being taken to resolve the issues. This kind of communication reassures users that their concerns are taken seriously and that the company is dedicated to delivering a quality product.

In healthcare, transparency is equally crucial. Doctors and medical professionals must communicate clearly about treatment plans and potential risks. When patients are fully informed, they can make educated decisions about their care. This trust can lead to better outcomes, as patients feel empowered and valued, ultimately fostering a stronger patient-provider relationship.

Similarly, in retail, clear communication about stock levels and delivery timelines can significantly enhance customer experience. For example, if a popular item is out of stock, informing customers about when they can expect it back on the shelves—or offering alternative products—demonstrates respect for their time and needs. This not only mitigates disappointment but can also create opportunities for upselling related items.

At the core of these examples is the idea that transparency is simply another word for honesty. It's essential to tell people the truth without being harsh. If you're going to be late, let them know and explain why. People appreciate honesty, especially when they understand that unforeseen issues can arise. Building an emotional bank account with your customers and employees is crucial. This means consistently providing excellent service and meeting expectations so that when problems do occur, you have plenty of goodwill saved up to draw from.

In essence, doing your job well and prioritizing customer service builds that "bank account." When challenges arise, this accumulated trust can help ensure you don't lose the customer's business. Remember, it's not just about what you say during good times; it's how you handle the tough situations that truly define your relationships and reputation. Transparency not only reinforces trust but also creates a solid foundation for lasting partnerships, allowing you to navigate the inevitable ups and downs of business with confidence.

Ultimately, the field of sales is about instilling confidence without arrogance. It's about acknowledging when you don't have the answers but promising to find them. It's about maintaining a sense of urgency and a commitment to resolving issues promptly. Above all, it's about treating every interaction and opportunity with the gravity it deserves.

So, how do you maintain a sense of urgency in your sales approach? Think of urgency as being personal. Consider your marriage: When your wife is unhappy, you quickly figure out how to fix the problem because you don't want to end up in bed with a frustrated partner. The same principle applies to your customers. If there's an issue, your goal should be to resolve it swiftly and effectively. This is crucial; I often get frustrated waiting for a callback. When I do follow up, I frequently hear, *"I was just about to call you"* or *"I'm sorry we've been so busy."* My response is always, *"You won't be too busy for long if I stop buying from you!"*

Urgency also ties into time management. By valuing your own time, you naturally cultivate a sense of urgency. If you hold your time in high regard, you'll likely do the same for your clients. When they see how you prioritize their time, it reinforces the importance of your relationship. Remember, time is one resource that, once lost, cannot be regained.

When I first started my business, people often remarked that my emails were curt and blunt. The reason was simple: I prefer straightforward communication. If you ask me for a yes or no answer, that's what you'll get—no lengthy explanations or unnecessary details. By keeping my responses brief, I save time for both myself and the recipient. Instead of crafting twenty-minute emails, I focus on delivering clear, concise answers that get straight to the point.

This principle extends to voicemail as well. I make it a point to leave short messages that get right to the heart of the matter. The only time I'll leave a longer voicemail is to explain why I'm calling, so if they return my call later, they'll know the context. After all, I may have called thirty people by then and might need a reminder!

By maintaining a sense of urgency in your communication and actions, you not only demonstrate respect for your clients' time but also foster a relationship built on trust and reliability. Remember, confidence in sales is about being proactive, responsive, and genuinely committed to solving your customers' needs.

Riding the Highs and Lows of Sales

Sales aren't confined to a single career path; you can sell anything—cars, real estate, pharmaceuticals—you name it. The key is mastering the craft of sales itself. So, how do you go about mastering this craft?

First and foremost, continuous learning is essential. Unfortunately, many salespeople overlook this aspect, but knowledge truly is power. If you strive to know more than anyone else in your industry—or at least make a consistent effort to get there—you position yourself as a leader in your field. Mastery comes from never stopping your pursuit of knowledge. Watch training videos, study successful salespeople, and read their books. Absorb their strategies and understand their approaches. There will always be valuable insights that can help you elevate your game.

However, it's crucial to keep learning at the forefront of your mind. Yes, many resources will reiterate the same fundamental principles, but the real danger lies in getting caught up in the day-to-day grind and losing sight of your growth. In the rush to secure the next order, you might forget to hone your skills. Remember, mastering a skill takes time and effort, so continuously working toward improvement is vital.

Here's an interesting tidbit: At one of the companies I worked for, we faced challenges in promoting outstanding salespeople to general manager positions because they were often reluctant to take a pay cut (their sales commissions had them making significantly more than a general manager's salary). This illustrates just how highly valued sales skills are—no fancy degrees are necessary, just a thirst for learning and a commitment to mastering your craft.

In summary, embrace the journey of continuous improvement. The more you invest in your knowledge and skills, the more successful you will become in your sales career.

Now, let's talk about the highs and lows of sales. The lows, in particular, can be brutal and often feel deeply personal. When there's a problem, it can weigh heavily on you, especially when you face multiple setbacks in a row. In those moments, it's essential to find a way to muscle through and stay focused on the next call. Creating a high sense of urgency helps manage these challenges; it's a crucial reason I encourage my team to prioritize solving issues quickly. No matter who makes a mistake within our organization, the impact can feel incredibly personal, and it drives me crazy.

One low I experienced early in my business was when I bid on a salt storage building in Maryland. Initially, it seemed like a straightforward project, and I was thrilled when I secured the job—especially since I had only been in business for a few months, and this was a sizable order for me. However, as we delved deeper into the design, it became clear that the project was far more complicated than anticipated. Ultimately, it ended up costing me $27,000 that I didn't have. This experience taught me a harsh lesson, and I've been more cautious with similar projects ever since.

Another challenging moment in my career occurred when I was aggressively trying to secure work. I was called into the vice president's office for a meeting, only to find a dissatisfied customer sitting there. They expressed their disappointment in my performance and requested a new salesperson. While I don't remember the specifics of what went wrong, I do recall the overwhelming feeling that I had taken this customer for granted. I didn't do a good job of nurturing that relationship, and I deserved the criticism.

These moments can either defeat you or inspire you. I won't pretend that I always came away inspired after getting my rear kicked, but eventually, you do have to own up to your mistakes. Even if you feel unjustly criticized, the customer's perception is what matters most. Accepting responsibility for their experience is the first step toward improvement and growth in this field.

The highs in sales can sometimes feel few and far between as we often navigate through many valleys before reaching those peaks. However, when those highs do come, they are incredibly sweet and should be cherished. Securing a significant sales order can be a thrilling experience, and receiving a phone call praising your work and your organization is a rare gem in this field. We all know such affirmations don't come often, but when they do, it's essential to hold onto them and let them fuel your motivation.

One of my greatest sources of joy comes from simply driving down the road and seeing our trucks loaded with trusses adorned with our logo. It reminds me of when I started Apex Truss, when I couldn't give work away. It's a constant reminder of how far we've come. I never lose sight of those early days, especially when someone asks what I do and responds with, *"Oh, I've heard of you! I see your trucks all over the road."* That recognition never gets old; it represents years of hard work and dedication finally paying off.

To create personal highs, I often reflect on my journey and where I started. The challenges I faced and the struggles I overcame make the success I experience now even sweeter. It's a comforting realization to know that despite the uncertainties of business, the progress I've made is monumental.

Sales is undoubtedly a rollercoaster ride, with the potential for multiple highs and lows in a single day. Few professions offer such dynamism. The beauty of this craft is that it only improves with time and experience. There's a wealth of resources available to help you refine your skills, making the journey not just about the destination but also about continuous growth and learning. Embracing both the highs and the lows is what makes this career truly rewarding.

Find Your People: Target Market

Not everyone is going to be lining up to buy what you're selling, and that's perfectly okay. The key is figuring out who will truly benefit from your product. Take a good look around—who's going to be blown away by what you offer? Once you've identified your target audience, it's all about speaking their language and demonstrating why they can't live without your solution. Below are some examples to illustrate how no matter what industry you work in, understanding your customers is crucial for success.

I love cars and know a fair bit about them, but I'm not a walking encyclopedia. When I walk into a dealership, especially for a car I'm interested in, I want to engage with a salesperson who truly knows their stuff. The best salespeople can knock your socks off with their extensive knowledge about the vehicle, making you feel like the only customer in the room. That personal connection can seal the deal. On the flip side, nothing frustrates me more than talking to a salesperson who knows less than I do about the car. When they fail to answer simple questions about legroom, engine size, or warranty details, it becomes painfully obvious they aren't putting in the effort. Too often, people think their product will sell itself, but that's a big mistake.

Think about the last time you shopped for clothes. When you walk into a store, do you want to be greeted by someone who knows the fabrics, styles, and fit? You bet! If a salesperson can suggest items to suit your style and body type, they're more likely to make a sale. It's about understanding what the customer wants and guiding them toward their perfect fit.

After years of going to different gyms, I finally decided to work out at home. I knew exactly what equipment I wanted—mostly bodyweight-focused, like pull-up bars and kettlebells. Every time I call my favorite equipment supplier, the person on the other end immediately understands what I need and helps me find the right gear. Their product knowledge and ability to cater to my specific setup have made me a loyal customer. With thousands of items in their inventory, I've never once spoken to someone who didn't know exactly what they were talking about.

When I stroll into a juice bar, I often don't know what I want. But a knowledgeable employee can change that. Instead of just waiting for my order, they'll ask me what I'm trying to achieve. If I express that I'm a picky eater who doesn't like chunks, they'll suggest options tailored to my preferences. It's a missed opportunity when staff fail to upsell based on a customer's needs. A good salesperson can turn a $6 drink into a $12 one by understanding what the customer wants and providing value. Upselling is key.

Real estate can be one of my biggest pet peeves. Too many agents seem incompetent, just throwing mud at the wall to see what sticks. However, the real pros are those who act with urgency and return calls promptly. They understand that the best deals often never hit the market. When an agent calls me to say, *"Hey, I have a property coming soon that fits what you're looking for,"* I'm more inclined to work with them. They're out there hustling for me, which is rare in this field. In real estate, saving even 5 percent on a million-dollar deal is significant, and those who are genuinely engaged make all the difference. As a realtor, find ways you can stand and be the best representative for your client.

To summarize this, knowing your target market means understanding who will resonate with your product and how to communicate effectively with them. It's about building relationships, demonstrating genuine knowledge, and showing that you care. When you find your people and speak their language, you set yourself up for success, regardless of your industry.

Build Relationships, Not Just Sales

Selling isn't just about making a quick buck; it's about creating a community. You want to treat your customers like they're part of the family, not just another transaction. Take the time to get to know them genuinely—ask about their day, remember their preferences, and show them you care. When people feel valued beyond the sale, they'll keep coming back and might even bring their friends along for the ride.

So, how do you build community? One effective strategy I employ is supporting local youth activities. Whenever possible, I back up any event involving kids, whether it's sports teams or school projects. I make sure to get my logo on their shirts or team apparel, fostering a sense of connection between my business and the community. It's important to be the company people think of first, especially in a niche like truss manufacturing.

This approach may seem small, but it pays off over time. As families see my commitment to supporting local kids, they begin to recognize my business as solid and community-focused. You never know who they might know or how that connection could influence future project recommendations. It's a long game, requiring consistency and patience, but the relationships built during this process can lead to significant opportunities down the road.

The Power of Connections in Sales

Connections are the lifeblood of any successful sales strategy. Building strong relationships can open doors to new opportunities, provide valuable insights, and create a network of support that propels you forward. When you cultivate genuine connections, you're not just expanding your circle; you're creating a foundation that can enhance your sales performance.

Why Connections Matter

1. **Trust and Credibility:** People are more likely to buy from someone they trust. Building connections allows you to establish rapport and credibility with your customers, making them feel more comfortable with your offerings.

2. **Referrals and Recommendations:** Satisfied customers are your best marketing tools. When you have strong connections, they're more likely to refer you to friends and colleagues, helping you grow your client base without spending a dime on advertising.

3. **Insights and Feedback:** Your connections can provide invaluable insights into market trends, customer preferences, and potential pain points. This information helps you tailor your sales approach and offerings to better meet the needs of your target audience.

4. **Opportunities for Collaboration:** Networking can lead to collaborations that benefit both parties. Whether it's partnering with other businesses for cross-promotions or collaborating on projects, these connections can expand your reach and enhance your credibility.

How to Use Connections to Advance in Sales

1. **Leverage Existing Relationships:** Don't hesitate to reach out to your current contacts. Inform them about your products or services and ask if they know anyone

who might benefit from what you offer. A simple conversation can lead to valuable introductions.

2. **Network Strategically:** Attend industry events, workshops, and seminars to meet new people. Make it a goal to connect with at least a few individuals at each event and follow up afterward to nurture those relationships.

3. **Utilize Social Media:** Platforms like LinkedIn can be powerful for building and maintaining connections. Share valuable content, engage with others' posts, and reach out to expand your network digitally.

4. **Offer Value First:** Before asking for something, consider how you can provide value to your connections. Share insights, offer your expertise, or simply lend an ear. When you help others, they'll be more inclined to return the favor.

5. **Listen Up, Talk Less:** As entrepreneur, businessman, and tire mogul Joe Tomarchio wisely said, *"If I had to change one thing, it's that I would listen more and talk less."* When engaging with potential clients, practice active listening. Ask open-ended questions and let them express their needs and concerns. This not only builds trust but also gives you crucial information to guide your sales pitch.

6. **Stay Consistent:** Building connections takes time and effort. Regularly check in with your contacts, share updates, and maintain relationships even when you don't need something from them. Consistency fosters loyalty and keeps you top-of-mind.

7. **Follow-up:** After meeting someone new or having a meaningful conversation, follow up with a thank-you message or a quick note. This reinforces your connection and keeps the lines of communication open.

Here are some practical tips for selling:

- **Know Your Product Inside and Out:** Understand every feature, benefit, and potential objection related to your product. This knowledge allows you to answer questions confidently and address concerns.
- **Understand Your Customer:** Research your target audience to understand their needs, pain points, and desires. Tailor your pitch to show how your product solves their specific problems.
- **Build Rapport:** Establish a connection with your customer. Use active listening, show genuine interest, and engage in small talk to make them feel comfortable and valued.
- **Ask Open-Ended Questions:** Encourage conversation by asking questions that require more than a yes or no answer. This helps you gather information and understand their perspective.
- **Communicate Value, Not Price:** Focus on the value your product brings rather than just its cost. Explain how it saves time, improves efficiency, or enhances their life, making the price seem justifiable.
- **Handle Objections Gracefully:** Anticipate objections and prepare thoughtful responses. Acknowledge their

concerns and provide reassurance, showing you're on their side.

- **Create a Sense of Urgency:** Encourage customers to act quickly by highlighting limited-time offers or the potential loss of a great opportunity. However, ensure any such urgency is genuine.
- **Follow-up:** If the customer doesn't decide immediately, follow up with them. A friendly reminder can keep your product top-of-mind and demonstrate your commitment.
- **Be Authentic:** People appreciate honesty and sincerity. Be yourself and let your passion for the product shine through. Authenticity builds trust.
- **Know Your Margins:** Understand your profit margins to ensure your sales efforts translate into actual profit. Selling at a loss can be detrimental in the long run.
- **Read the Room:** Pay attention to your customers' body language and reactions. Adapting your approach based on their responses can significantly improve your effectiveness.
- **Empathy:** Put yourself in each customer's shoes. Understanding their emotions and perspectives can help you connect on a deeper level and tailor your pitch more effectively.
- **Continuous Learning:** Stay updated on sales techniques, market trends, and customer preferences. Regularly refine your skills and adapt your approach based on feedback and experience.

By combining these tips with a genuine belief in what you're selling, you can enhance your sales effectiveness and build lasting relationships with your customers.

"Those who work their land will have abundant food,
but those who chase fantasies have no sense."
~ Proverbs 12:11 (NIV) ~

Chapter 7

DECISION MAKING IN BUSINESS

The Tough Choices

"Whether you turn to the right or to the left, your ears will hear a voice behind you, saying, 'This is the way; walk in it.'"
~ Isaiah 30:21 (NIV) ~

Decision-making in business can feel like walking a tightrope—one wrong step and the whole operation can come crashing down. Every entrepreneur faces this reality: Your decisions can impact not only your business's bottom line but also the lives of your employees, customers, and even your family. Sometimes, these choices will make you the hero in your own story; other times, they may paint you as the villain. But at the end of the day, you must do what's best for your business, which often means making tough calls.

In decision-making, especially when faced with tough choices, listening to that inner guidance is vital, trusting that you are being led in the right direction. Just as the scripture reminds us, we will hear a voice guiding us on which path to take. Staying true to our values and instincts can help illuminate the way when the road ahead seems unclear.

Let's face it: not everyone will agree with your decisions. In fact, in every industry, you're bound to ruffle some feathers. For instance, consider a manufacturing business that needs to cut costs to stay competitive. The decision to lay off a few employees, while necessary for the financial health of the company, can leave lasting scars. Those who are let go may see you as the "bad guy," and even those who remain might feel a sense of unease about their own job security.

In the retail sector, imagine a store manager who must choose between raising prices or reducing staff hours to maintain profitability. Raising prices might alienate loyal customers while cutting hours could demoralize employees and impact service quality. The pressure is immense, and the stakes are high.

In tech, a founder may face the hard choice of pivoting the company's focus. This decision could mean abandoning a beloved product some customers cherish. The backlash from devoted users can be swift and harsh, branding you as someone out of touch with your audience. Yet, it may be a necessary step to ensure long-term growth and survival in a rapidly changing market.

Navigating the highs and lows is a tricky part of any entrepreneur's life. You've got to build calluses for this journey. Think about it: You're either entering the valley of the abyss or climbing out of it. Your peaks are often narrow and short-lived, which means you'll constantly feel some strain—whether you're going down or coming up. If you visualize this journey like a mountain, you'll see that the peaks are small, but the valleys are deep.

Over time, life's erosion will help you create trails to navigate the pitfalls of your journey. I once went on an adventure in the Great Mine ruins, where a rope led to the top of a pyramid. My two kids and I climbed to the summit, each step requiring careful consideration due to the ancient structure's condition. Upon reaching the top, I looked down and thought, "What have I done?" Suddenly, I had to navigate back down with my kids behind me, praying that no one above us would stumble and us all falling like bowling pins. This is very much how the entrepreneurial journey feels: You climb to the top only to realize you must descend again. As you repeat this process, you develop a trail and calluses that help you manage the arduous journey.

While it may feel uncomfortable to make decisions that can be perceived negatively, it's crucial to remember that leadership often requires a level of detachment. You have to evaluate situations based on data, potential outcomes, and what's best for your organization's future, not just what's popular at the moment.

Examples of Tough Decisions Across Industries

1. **Manufacturing:** A factory might need to automate specific processes to stay competitive. While this decision can improve efficiency and reduce costs, it also means eliminating jobs. A good leader must communicate transparently about why these changes

are happening and what support will be provided for affected employees.

2. **Retail:** During a downturn, a retailer may need to close underperforming locations. This decision can hurt communities and local employees, but it is essential for overall viability. The approach should include outreach to those affected and perhaps offering them opportunities at nearby locations.

3. **Healthcare:** A hospital director may need to make cuts to specific departments due to budget constraints. This can lead to pushback from staff and community members. Engaging with all stakeholders to discuss the reasons for and potential impacts on patient care can help mitigate the backlash.

4. **Tech Startups:** A founder might need to decide to pivot from a project that's consuming resources without yielding results. This can mean disappointing investors and team members. Communicating the rationale behind the shift and the potential for future success can help retain trust and morale.

The Emotional Toll of Decision-Making

Making tough decisions is taxing on the emotional side of business. Others may second-guess you, but they see only a low elevation. You, however, are higher up and understand the broader view of what's happening. I remember my early days running my first truss plant. I was young and still learning to manage people. The guy I replaced was older and more experienced, and he didn't like me much. After months of navigating the situation, I reached my breaking point and moved him into a cubicle, creating a rift between us. One day, I called him into my office and laid it out clearly. I told him to visualize two rams standing on hillsides, heading for a collision at the bottom. *"I know which one will be standing,"* I said, pointing at myself. He quit six weeks later, and I realized that sometimes you have to be firm to hold fast to your vision for the company.

How to Make Tough Decisions

1. **Gather Data:** The first step in making any tough decision is to gather as much relevant information as possible. Understand the financials, market trends, and customer feedback.

2. **Consider the Long-Term Impact:** Think about how your decision will affect the business in the long run. Will it lead to growth? Will it improve customer satisfaction?

3. **Consult with Others:** Don't hesitate to seek input from trusted advisors, mentors, or team members. Different perspectives can shed light on aspects you may not have considered.

4. **Make a Pros and Cons List:** Writing down the benefits and drawbacks of your potential choices can clarify your thinking. This method also makes it easier to communicate your reasoning to others later on.

5. **Be Transparent:** When announcing your decision, be clear about your reasoning. Transparency can help

alleviate some concerns and fears, even if people disagree with your decision.

6. **Prepare for Backlash:** Understand that not everyone will be happy with your decision. Prepare to face criticism and have a plan for addressing concerns from employees, customers, and stakeholders.

7. **Stay Firm but Fair:** Once you've made your decision, stick to it. However, be open to feedback and willing to adapt if new information arises.

8. **Learn from Experience:** Every decision provides an opportunity to learn. After implementing your decision, reflect on its outcomes. What went well? What didn't? Use these insights for future decision-making.

Ultimately, being a leader means accepting that some decisions will be challenging and may even lead to negative perceptions. But remember, as long as you're making decisions based on sound reasoning and what's best for the business, you can stand by your choices.

Keep in mind that the entrepreneurial journey is rarely smooth sailing. There will be rough waters, and there will be times when you have to make tough decisions that could upset people. But that's part of the territory. As you navigate these challenges, always prioritize your vision and purpose for your business.

Your ability to make tough decisions will define not only your business's success but also your growth as a leader. So, don't shy away from the hard choices. Embrace them, learn from them, and let them guide you to greater heights. In the end, every decision you make is a step toward building the legacy you aspire to create.

"There is a time for everything, and a season for every activity under the heavens."
~ Ecclesiastes 3:1 (NIV) ~

Chapter 8

BUILDING
YOUR EMPIRE

*"Therefore everyone who hears these words of mine and puts them into
practice is like a wise man who built his house on the rock. The rain came
down, the streams rose, and the winds blew and beat against that house;
yet it did not fall, because it had its foundation on the rock."*
~ *Matthew 7:24-25 (NIV)* ~

In the entrepreneurial world, building your empire isn't just
about making money; it's about creating something that
lasts—a legacy that extends beyond your immediate
influence. Whether you're just starting out or you've been in
business for a while, the ability to expand and grow is crucial
for long-term success. So here are some strategies you can
use to build your empire, whether you're looking to scale up
your current business or lay the groundwork for future
growth.

The principle of building on a strong foundation is crucial to
entrepreneurship, just as it is in life. As the above scripture
illustrates, a solid foundation is what allows us to withstand
the challenges that come with building something great. In
business, that foundation is built on sound principles,

perseverance, and the right mindset—things that will ensure you remain standing even when the storm hits.

Creating a Micro-Monopoly

Creating a micro-monopoly is about dominating a small market and keeping even the biggest players out. While many entrepreneurs chase the allure of scaling because, let's face it, that seems sexy, there's immense value in being a local powerhouse. Local businesses allow for personal connections within the community that are hard to break. Relationships matter.

We've been conditioned to believe that bigger is better, often using giants like Amazon and Walmart as examples. However, this mindset has led us to accept poor service as the norm, which is simply unacceptable. It's frustrating to call a company and feel like you're begging them to take your money just to receive basic service. It's time to turn this around and focus on what can be accomplished at a local level.

Consider this: The top 1 percent earn around $540,000 a year, including in some of the most expensive markets. If you make $400,000 a year in a place like Waco, Texas, you're doing exceptionally well; in a place like Washington, DC, that same income might barely keep you afloat. Being a big fish in a small pond has its advantages; you can make a real impact on people's lives with simple acts of help without needing to create grand gestures like building wings on hospitals.

Building strong relationships with local banks is crucial. Larger banks often only care about big deals, which means smaller businesses may struggle to get the attention they deserve. As these banks grow, it will become even harder for smaller players to secure support. Focus on cultivating those local connections, as they can provide invaluable resources and support that larger institutions overlook.

I encourage everyone to establish superb financial tracking from the very start of their business. Set up your financials with balance sheets, receivables, payables, and cash flow projections. Don't try to do this on the fly; it will only lead to chaos. Be quick to invoice and aggressive in collecting payments. I've done over $120 million in sales over the last two decades and have written off less than $60,000 in bad debt.

If you don't understand financials, learn. Hire a competent medium-sized accounting firm rather than relying on a part-time bookkeeper. Otherwise, you will get too busy to keep an eye on your finances. I review my payables, receivables, and financials every day, and I don't let anyone else sign my checks. I've learned from experience that people can get lazy, leading to losses. You need to be vigilant—every penny counts in the early days, just like it does in any well-run business.

At some point, you'll want to borrow money from the bank, and having excellent financials, even if they show a loss, will give you credibility. My banks have often remarked how they wish every company my size had the reporting systems I do.

By reviewing my finances daily, sometimes multiple times, I can catch trends and minimize mistakes.

The financial side can be intimidating, but I urge you to embrace it. It's not that hard to learn. If you have questions, Google them or consult your accountant. Don't stick your head in the sand and ignore the reality of your situation. Remember, no one will watch your money better than you will. If you're unsure about something, have a meeting with your accountant. It may cost a few hundred dollars, but it will save you much more in the long run.

I use QuickBooks and know it inside and out, right down to every journal entry. I set up every financial P&L from the beginning. It doesn't matter if you're a salesman, engineer, or just starting out—you *must always* know where your money is going. If you neglect this, you'll regret it when it's too late.

Once you become comfortable with your financial systems, it won't take much time. I spend just ten to fifteen minutes a day reviewing my financials. This allows me to catch discrepancies and keep my team accountable. Remember, your employees will take little things—time, supplies, anything they can. Watching trends from the beginning helps you catch the small issues before they become big problems.

Building a sustainable business requires you to act like you're always broke, even when you're not. You must understand inventory turns, payables, receivables, and cash flow. If you struggle with these concepts, establish procedures and policies that protect you. Learn to file information so that you can locate it quickly and efficiently.

Setting the Stage for Expansion

If you're already in business, the first step to expansion is assessing your current operations. What's working? What's not? Are you maximizing your resources? Here's how to begin:

- **Evaluate Your Current Business Model:** Before you can expand, you need a solid understanding of your current operations. Conduct a thorough analysis of your business model, including your target market, customer feedback, and financial performance. Identify areas where you can improve efficiency or enhance customer satisfaction.
- **Create a Clear Vision:** To grow your empire, you need to have a vision of what that looks like. What do you want to achieve? Whether it's increasing revenue, expanding your product line, or entering new markets, your vision should be clear and compelling. It will serve as your north star as you navigate the complexities of growth.

Planning for Expansion

If you're starting a new business, you have a unique advantage: the opportunity to plan for expansion from the ground up. Here's how:

- **Develop a Scalable Business Plan:** When creating your business plan, think about scalability. How can you design your operations so that they can grow without a hitch? This may involve automating certain processes, outsourcing tasks, or investing in technology that can handle increased demand. Make sure your plan outlines both short-term and long-term goals, with milestones to track your progress.

- **Build a Strong Brand Identity:** Your brand is your empire's foundation. A strong, recognizable brand identity will help you attract and retain customers, making it easier to expand. Ensure your branding is consistent across all channels—website, social media, packaging, and customer interactions. A well-defined brand will make it easier to market new products or services in the future.

Strategies for Expansion

Now that you're grounded in your current business or laying the foundation for a new one let's explore some specific strategies for expansion:

- **Diversify Your Offerings:** One way to expand your business is by diversifying your product or service offerings. This can involve introducing complementary products, bundling services, or expanding into new categories that align with your brand. Diversification helps you tap into new revenue streams while also offering more value to your existing customers.

- **Consider Franchising:** If your business model is replicable, franchising can be an excellent option for expansion. This allows you to leverage the investment and efforts of franchisees while maintaining control over your brand and operations. However, be prepared to invest time and resources into creating a robust franchise system, including training, support, and marketing materials.
- **Explore Partnerships and Collaborations:** Strategic partnerships can help you reach new markets and expand your offerings without the overhead of opening new locations or developing new products from scratch. Collaborate with complementary businesses to create bundled offerings or co-host events that attract your target audience.
- **Invest in Marketing:** As you expand, your marketing efforts should also grow. Use digital marketing strategies to reach new customers—think SEO, social media advertising, and email campaigns. Consider leveraging influencers or affiliate marketing to tap into new audiences. Always measure the effectiveness of your marketing campaigns and adjust your strategy based on data-driven insights.

Now, let's talk about the rollercoaster ride of entrepreneurship. Navigating the highs and lows is a challenging part of any entrepreneur's life. You must build calluses to understand that when you think about it, you're either entering the valley of the abyss or coming out of it. Your peaks are often narrow and short-lived, which means you'll constantly experience some form of strain—whether going down or coming up. In other words, If you visualize this journey like a standard mountain, you'll see that the peaks are small, but the valleys are deep.

Selling Your Business

At some point, you might decide to sell your business. Whether it's to cash in on your hard work or to move on to your next adventure, selling requires careful planning:

- **Prepare for Sale Early:** If you think you might sell your business one day, start preparing now. Build a solid financial history, streamline operations, and maintain clean records. A business with a proven track record and efficient operations is more attractive to potential buyers.
- **Determine Your Valuation:** Understanding your business's value is crucial when you're ready to sell. Consult with a business valuation expert to assess your company's worth. Consider factors like profitability, growth potential, and market trends to determine a fair price.

Transitioning Leadership

As your empire grows, there may come a time when you want to step back and let someone else take the reins. Here's how to make that transition smoothly:

- **Identify a Successor:** When considering stepping down, look for someone within your organization who shares your vision and values. This could be a current employee, a manager, or even a trusted colleague from outside your business. Make sure they are equipped with the skills and experience necessary to lead effectively.

- **Create a Succession Plan:** A well-defined succession plan is essential for a smooth transition. This plan should outline the new leader's roles and responsibilities, as well as any necessary training or mentorship to prepare them for their new position. To maintain stability within the organization, the transition should be gradual.

- **Communicate Clearly:** Transparency is key during any leadership transition. Communicate your decision to your team and stakeholders clearly, explaining the reasons for the change and what they can expect moving forward. This will help maintain trust and morale within the organization.

Building your empire is a journey filled with challenges and triumphs. Whether you're expanding your existing business or starting anew, remember that growth requires strategic planning, a clear vision, and a willingness to adapt. Embrace the journey and know the road ahead will shape not only your business but also the legacy you leave behind. Your empire awaits—go build it!

In my experience, I've learned that while I may not be the most organized person, I have surrounded myself with people who are. I spend time each and every day reviewing my financial data, understanding it better than anyone else in my company. Remember, you're making decisions based on the big picture, while your employees are often focused on immediate issues. You must look weeks ahead to anticipate what's coming.

Managing resources effectively means acknowledging that others may think they know better than you. Be okay with that; it's just how it is. I worked for someone who I thought I was smarter than, only to realize I had a lot to learn once I started my own business. Pay attention to the lessons around you and understand that education is a continuous journey in entrepreneurship.

In our fast-paced society, many expect instant results, like instant oatmeal. However, true success requires patience and time, just like traditional oatmeal, which needs proper cooking. You must embrace the process and understand that quick fixes often lead to superficial outcomes.

In the wild ride we call life, you've got to adopt a "whatever it takes" attitude. It's not always pretty, but finding the silver lining in every situation is crucial. Even when you feel like you're lost in the dark, there's always a star shining somewhere, reminding you that hope exists. The constant pursuit of winning can be brutal, no doubt about it. Risk? It's scary as hell. But when you finally land that win? Oh boy, it's a feeling like no other!

Now, let me tell you, you're going to face more losses than wins, and that's just the reality of entrepreneurship. I remember borrowing $50,000 from my parents to buy a vending route. For three long years, I filled those machines, and let me tell you, it was humbling. Do you think you know humility? Try dealing with customers who'll bust your chops over a sixty-five-cent bag of expired chips. They'll toss it on the counter, but you better believe they'll munch down every single damn bag anyway! It's eye-opening to see how people act when they think you're just a vending machine filler. You learn a lot about the human condition when you're in that position.

There I was, taking calls from vendors who were demanding their money while I was in between stops. It was a brutal time, and at one point, I felt like I was drowning. But I kept grinding because I was on a mission. I sold that business for $90,000, paid my parents back, and made a tidy $40,000 profit. The guy I bought the route from, the biggest vending company in the area, told me I was the only one he ever sold a route to who actually made it and sold it at a profit. That was a badge of honor for me.

I was just a good man trying to survive, doing whatever it took to provide for my family—one nickel, dime, quarter, and dollar at a time—without going bankrupt in the process. People have no idea how tough it is. They only see the glossy surface, the perceived ease of success, and think you got lucky. Ever wonder if you weren't meant to be successful? I'm here to tell you that mindset needs to change.

I remember cleaning buildings at night just to buy our first house. That wasn't glamorous, but it was part of the grind. Every scrubbing session, every late night, was a stepping stone to something better.

The *"whatever it takes"* mantra isn't just about pushing through; it's about understanding how the struggle is part of the journey. Every setback is a lesson, every failure an opportunity to grow. So, embrace the hustle, adapt to the challenges, and keep your eyes on the prize. When the going gets tough, remember that the only way to get ahead is to dig deep and find that inner drive. Trust me, the victories taste so much sweeter when you've worked your ass off to earn them.

Fear of Failure: The Driving Force

Let's get one thing straight: fear can be your ally if you let it. Fear of failure should be the fuel that propels you forward, igniting a fire in your belly. When you miss the mark, use that feeling to drive you toward the next opportunity. Some days, it might feel like you're stumbling, but those are the days when you need to grab hold of your bootstraps and keep moving forward. Remember, losses make the wins that much sweeter.

You'll never be short on people who tell you, *"You can't do it."* Misery loves company, and the only one at your pity party should be you. Blow out those candles and embrace the challenge. There's a reason most folks work for someone else: They're scared to take risks. But I was determined to work for myself, and that fire drove me hard. Now, I can't imagine working for anyone else.

We've created a society that hands out trophies just for showing up. Second place gets a trophy, and first place? Well, they hardly even get a nod these days. You might go through your entire journey with little recognition, but when you stumble and fall flat on your face, trust me, there'll be a stadium full of onlookers. Let that drive you to dust yourself off and get back in the game. Remember, everyone in that stadium paid to be there, and they're just watching. You're not a spectator; you want to be on the field fighting for the win. Those spectators? They're sheep.

Fear of failure has fueled me through some of my darkest moments. I found myself $2.2 million in the hole, and everything around me screamed to quit. But I chose to keep going. I was so broke that I couldn't even declare bankruptcy, so in my mind, the only way out was up. I had a friend who went bankrupt twenty years ago, and he never bounced back. It's sad to see, especially since he was a genuinely nice guy.

You will face failures, but the choice is yours: Let them defeat you or use them to fuel your motivation. I chose to be inspired, not defeated. When you feel like you're down for the count, remember you're aiming for long-term wealth, not just a quick buck. Everything in this game is a choice, and you're the one in control of those choices—no one else.

Fear can motivate you if you learn to channel it. Society has programmed us to be weak, making it easy for them to control us. Listen, it's simple: A weak society is easily manipulated. So, don't let yourself be part of that. Find the positives, even when life throws you a curveball. As Kenny Rogers said in his song "The Greatest," it's about finding the silver lining, even when the world is trying to label it a loss. Remember, every setback can be a setup for your next comeback. Keep pushing, keep fighting, and don't let fear hold you back!

> "Enlarge the place of your tent, stretch
> your tent curtains wide,
> do not hold back; lengthen your cords,
> strengthen your stakes."
> ~ Isaiah 54:2 (NIV) ~

Chapter 9

THE ENTREPRENEUR'S CODE AND THE UNWRITTEN RULES OF THE TOP 1%: INTEGRITY, LEADERSHIP, AND RESPONSIBILITY. DO WHAT'S RIGHT!

"For we are taking pains to do what is right, not only in the eyes of the Lord but also in the eyes of man."
~ 2 Corinthians 8:21 (NIV) ~

Integrity is a topic that often goes unspoken in the world of business, yet it's crucial. I've trademarked the phrase *Do What's Right* because I believe it encapsulates a principle I strive to live by, both in life and in my business. While I haven't always succeeded, I've learned valuable lessons through my mistakes.

For instance, during the financial crisis of 2010, I faced a tempting offer from a manufacturing company that sold plates at nearly half the market price. Despite my initial research showing many companies doing the same, I justified this decision to myself for months. When I eventually got caught, the embarrassment was overwhelming. I knew it was wrong, but I let my guard down. Just because others were doing it didn't make it right, and I regret exposing myself to such weakness.

I made another error by allowing my ego to cloud my judgment. After years of success, I was bragging about a significant decision to a few acquaintances, believing it wouldn't come back to haunt me. I was mistaken, and it bit me hard. The lesson? Keep your mouth shut unless you're prepared for the consequences. If you die with only two or three close friends, you've truly succeeded.

In business, maintaining integrity and character is paramount. You must take responsibility for your actions and move forward, even if it takes time. Success can make you blind to your decisions, but if you have integrity, it will nag at you, as it should. A wise man once told me that if I have to make someone feel bad for their mistakes, they shouldn't be working for me. This applies to self-reflection as well. God isn't going to ask for your bank balance when you get there. So, don't just chase a quick buck.

We all make mistakes; it's part of the journey. It's not the mistakes that define you but how you handle them. If you think you have everything figured out at twenty years old, speak to someone who's sixty—they'll set you straight. Habits can destroy you, and if you let negativity take root, you'll regret it.

People often talk, and news travels fast. If you have a reputation for lacking integrity, it will follow you. You might not care what others think, but remember: What goes around comes around. Many with bad intentions may seem to succeed in the short term, but in the long run, their lack of integrity will catch up with them.

A pivotal moment for me occurred when I met with the owner of a company that provided materials for my business. He wanted to learn my story and understand Apex. Despite his intimidating reputation, our meeting was productive. In the end, he expressed his intention to work with me, and I've been purchasing materials from them ever since. This relationship was built on trust and integrity, proving that others will reciprocate when you uphold your word.

Throughout my career, I've faced financial difficulties, and one thing I've learned is the importance of communication. Always return calls from those who are owed money. Being upfront and honest helps maintain relationships. If you promise to mail a check, do it. When I owed American Express a significant sum, I initially avoided their calls. But when I finally answered, we were able to work out a plan. Ignoring problems won't solve them; you must face your challenges head-on.

In summary, the entrepreneur's code is built on integrity, responsibility, and the relationships you cultivate. These principles will not only guide you through tough times but will also leave a lasting legacy that speaks volumes about who you are as a person and a business leader.

As I reflect on my life and career, the concept of legacy weighs heavily on my mind. The truth is no one can fully predict what their legacy will be. It's a daunting thought. Each time I hear someone speak about the nice things said about a person after they've passed, I can't help but think that these words should be shared while they're still alive. The essence of a legacy is not just in what we leave behind but in how we touch the lives of those around us during our journey.

From a young age, my perspective on legacy has evolved dramatically. Initially, my focus was on achieving personal success, but over the years, I've come to realize that the most meaningful legacy is one that impacts others—especially young people. Their minds are still malleable, open to influence, and capable of being shaped. While I've consistently changed and grown, I recognize that many people become set in their ways as they age. Yet, as entrepreneurs, we often possess the capacity for adaptability, driven by our experiences and the challenges we face.

In 2018, I took on an ambitious project: writing one hundred and twenty-two blogs in a row. The motivation behind this endeavor was simple: I wanted my children to understand my thoughts and motivations. Fast-forward six years, and as I work on this book, my focus has shifted to my grandchildren. I want them to know who I was, see my picture on the wall, and understand the values I held dear.

Ultimately, I aspire to be remembered as a kind person with unwavering integrity—someone who wasn't always right but was always willing to admit when he was wrong and to apologize. This commitment to authenticity is a cornerstone of the legacy I hope to leave behind.

As I grow older, the importance of making a lasting impression on my grandchildren has become increasingly clear. I want them to reflect on my life and say, *"My grandfather helped me,"* even after I'm gone. If we're fortunate, our presence will linger as just a photograph on a wall, cherished for a generation. Yet, I find it bittersweet that none of my grandchildren truly know my father-in-law, a remarkable man who profoundly influenced my life. His legacy lives on, but the details have faded, reminding me of the urgency to create a lasting impact.

In essence, leaving a legacy is about more than just memories; it's about forging connections and imparting wisdom that can guide future generations. As I navigate this journey, I remain committed to ensuring that my actions today will echo in the lives of those I love tomorrow.

I'm willing to put in the effort that others aren't. As I often say in my book, everyone wants what you have; they just aren't willing to go through what it takes to get it. I'm a sixty-year-old overnight success, and I can assure you that those making real money aren't sitting down for dinner at 5:00 PM, watching the news, and heading to bed early. They're up before dawn, hustling late into the night, doing whatever it takes to get ahead.

So, remember this as you read my book: If you're lounging on the couch at 5:30, you're not getting into that elite club of the top 1 percent. Sure, there's always that one person who hits a home run and knocks it out of the park, but they're few and far between. If you think their lives are all sunshine and roses because of their Instagram posts, think again. The reality can be extremely tough. What sets them apart is their ability to maintain a positive attitude, put in the hard work, and turn their defeats into motivation.

That's the entrepreneurial spirit. What's hard is that when you're not yet making the big bucks, it can take years to see results. Very few achieve that success quickly. For every success story you see, there are years of struggle hidden behind it. I've had countless moments when I honestly didn't know if I would make payroll. People look at me now and say, *"Wow, you're so successful,"* but I'm acutely aware that I could be broke next year. That's why I stay sharp and never let my guard down.

Getting comfortable can lead to complacency, and trust me, if you get complacent, you're going to get punched in the face—and it's going to hurt. I know this from firsthand experience. In all my writings, I make a commitment to myself: I will never let that happen again. I don't hold grudges, but I never forget because when I screw up, it usually stings a lot. So, embrace that pain, learn from it, and turn it into gain.

In entrepreneurship, the toughest opponent you'll ever face is yourself. Seriously, that internal battle is often way more challenging than anything the outside world can throw at you. It's about getting out of your own way, mastering the roller coaster of ups and downs, and building that rock-solid confidence in your abilities. Remember, when you throw yourself a pity party, you're the only one who shows up.

We all wrestle with our inner demons. One minute, I'm feeling like the best in the game, and the next, I'm doubting everything. It's a wild ride, and honestly, it's not just me. I see folks all around who avoid taking chances because they fear disappointment, yet they end up disappointed for never taking the leap. It's a catch twenty-two that traps too many.

Fishing is a great metaphor here. Everyone loves to fish and catch fish, but they call it fishing for a reason—it's not always about the catch. Sometimes, you've got to cast your line and see what bites. Taking calculated risks is crucial. I'm not talking about reckless behavior; I mean having the confidence to pursue opportunities while being grounded enough to know when to reel it back in.

Let's face it: You may never fully figure yourself out, so don't expect to understand everyone else, either. I've got thin skin, and I often take things personally, which pushes me to toughen up. But it's a struggle, and I still find myself questioning what I want to be when I grow up, even at this stage in my life.

The key to overcoming this internal struggle is self-awareness. You have to recognize your strengths and weaknesses. What drives you? What holds you back? If you can't pinpoint these aspects, you're just wandering aimlessly. Take the time to reflect, write things down, or even talk it out with someone you trust.

Another crucial element is surrounding yourself with the right people. You want a team that uplifts you and challenges you to be better. When you've got a solid support system, it becomes easier to confront your fears. Those folks are your sounding board when you're unsure and your cheerleaders when you're on a roll.

Set realistic goals and celebrate the small wins along the way. Too often, we fixate on the big picture, and when we don't achieve it immediately, we feel defeated. But each step forward is progress, and acknowledging that helps build the confidence you need to keep pushing. It's all part of the journey.

And let's talk about resilience. You'll encounter setbacks; it's part of the game. But how you respond to those setbacks defines your character. Instead of sulking, use those moments as fuel. Learn from them, adapt, and bounce back stronger. Every failure is a lesson in disguise.

Moreover, don't be afraid to step out of your comfort zone. Growth happens when you challenge yourself. Whether it's trying a new approach in your business or tackling a personal fear, embrace the discomfort. That's where the magic happens.

Finally, embrace a mindset of continuous learning. The more you know, the more confident you'll be. Dive into books, podcasts, or courses—whatever it takes to expand your knowledge. The world is full of information just waiting for you to grab it, and that can turn the tide in your favor.

The most significant battle in your entrepreneurial journey is the one within. Confronting your fears, recognizing your weaknesses, and building resilience will set you on the path to success. Remember, you're not alone in this struggle; we all face it. So, put on your game face, face yourself head-on, and get ready to conquer your greatest enemy—yourself.

"In everything set them an example by doing what is good. In your teaching show integrity, seriousness, and soundness of speech that cannot be condemned, so that those who oppose you may be ashamed because they have nothing bad to say about us."
~ Titus 2:7-8 (NIV) ~

Chapter 10

THE BORN VS. MADE PARADOX

"Do you see someone skilled in their work? They will serve
before kings; they will not serve before officials of low rank."
~ Proverbs 22:29 (NIV) ~

As I've walked this entrepreneurial path, I often ponder whether we're born with certain qualities or shaped by our experiences. Are successful entrepreneurs wired with a unique set of traits, or do life's ups and downs mold them into the tenacious individuals we admire? The reality is that it's likely a mix of both nature and nurture.

This scripture beautifully ties into the paradox of whether entrepreneurs are born or made. Just as each person is uniquely gifted with certain strengths, these gifts shape our paths in different ways. The combination of our inherent qualities and the experiences we go through form the basis for our entrepreneurial journey, where each trait contributes to the greater purpose of our success.

Let's kick this off by looking at some traits that are typically associated with successful entrepreneurs. You can probably name a few of them: determination, resilience, and a clear vision. These qualities often show up early in life. Think about that kid who takes charge on the playground, organizing games and rallying friends for a cause. That's a glimpse of the entrepreneurial spirit in action. Take the story of a ten-year-old kid who decides to sell lemonade. While his friends are out playing, he's busy drafting a business plan, setting prices, and experimenting with flavors. This kind of ambition suggests a natural inclination toward entrepreneurship, but let's be clear: having these traits doesn't guarantee success.

Entrepreneurs have this unique mix of traits and mindsets that set them apart from the crowd. First up is adaptability. In this business game, things change faster than a New York minute, and if you can't pivot when new info comes in or when the market shifts, you're gonna be left in the dust. It's like being a seasoned sailor who knows how to adjust their sails when the winds change. You can't stick to one course and expect to get anywhere. This flexibility allows entrepreneurs to spot opportunities others might just overlook, keeping their businesses relevant and competitive.

Next, we can't forget about creativity. Entrepreneurs aren't just your run-of-the-mill problem solvers; they're innovators who see opportunities where others see roadblocks. They tackle challenges with an open mind, thinking outside the box to find unique solutions. This creativity bleeds into every part of their business, whether it's developing a killer product or coming up with a marketing strategy that turns heads. Picture a tech entrepreneur launching an app that makes life easier or a restaurant owner creating a dining experience so unique that customers can't help but keep coming back. It's that willingness to innovate that sets successful entrepreneurs apart.

Then there's risk-taking, which is essential. Let's face it: Every opportunity comes with its own set of risks. But instead of running from it, successful entrepreneurs embrace it. I'm not saying they're reckless; they just know how to weigh potential rewards against the downsides. This mindset opens the door to exploring new territories and tackling ambitious projects that could yield significant returns. Think of it like climbing a mountain: You might not know exactly what you're gonna face, but man, that view from the top makes it all worthwhile.

Of all the people I interviewed, Dianette Wells (elite mountaineer, adventure racer, and seven-summits climber), was the only one who answered the question of whether we're born or made in a very definitive way. She simply said, "Born. 100%."

And yet, while some folks might be born with a knack for leadership or a taste for risk, their environment plays a massive role in shaping their entrepreneurial mindset. Supportive families, mentors, and communities can foster resilience and encourage risk-taking, while negative experiences can instill doubt and hesitation.

Take, for instance, a young woman raised in a family of small business owners. She witnessed firsthand the struggles and victories that come with running a business. Seeing her parents navigate financial hurdles and learn from their mistakes instilled in her the belief that failure is just a stepping stone to growth. Armed with this mindset, she stepped into her own entrepreneurial journey, tackling challenges with unwavering determination. Her story shows that while innate qualities matter, they can be refined through experience.

Here's how one person I interviewed, Jack Daly (owner and CEO of TRX®, the market leader in Suspension Training) put it:

> We are definitely born with some foundational skills, and everybody has different skills and different levels of skills, but what you do with those is made. You can have great capabilities and wildly underperform versus those capabilities. You can also have very modest capabilities and wildly outperform those modest capabilities, right? I'm blessed with kids from the neighborhood, like a bunch of kids from Pittsburgh. I look at my friends, oh my gosh, a Navy Seal for 30 years, the top spine surgeon on the West Coast, a Hollywood mogul, a guy who runs a major hedge fund, and so on. Those are the kids I was running with and trying to keep up with, and I've been trying to keep up with them for six decades now, right? And so that's made; that's being surrounded by a group of people that you're benefiting from the relationship with them, and it's motivating, inspirational, and aspirational. They're encouraging you, they're helping you out. So, and I do think that family structure and the community you come from, I think makes it much more made.

Reality TV star Rachel Reilly Villegas also leans toward made:

> I think we're all a little bit made. For me especially, I didn't have a plan. I just kind of, follow what my heart tells me and take my journey a day at a time and try to live in the present. So, I think I'm probably made. I think that I build off of my past experiences, learn from my failures, and continue on life's journey, wherever it shall take me.

Type A personality traits are often linked to successful entrepreneurs, and I'm one of them. We folks have fierce determination and don't take "no" for an answer. We'll climb mountains, both literally and metaphorically, even after facing setbacks. What fuels this relentless drive? It's a mix of passion, purpose, and an unshakeable belief in our vision.

For many Type A personalities, failure isn't a setback—it's a challenge to tackle. We see obstacles as opportunities to innovate and adapt. This mindset often comes from formative experiences where we learn to face adversity head-on. Whether it's a childhood failure in sports or a tough grade in school, these experiences can stoke the flames of resilience.

Imagine a young entrepreneur facing rejection after rejection while seeking funding for his startup. Instead of throwing in the towel, he analyzes the feedback, tweaks his pitch, and explores alternative funding sources. This tenacity isn't just personality; it's a behavior cultivated through experience and a supportive environment that stresses persistence.

Now, let's talk about having a growth mindset. Entrepreneurs who succeed don't let failures knock them down. They see setbacks as lessons rather than defeats. When they face rejection or a failed venture, they don't throw in the towel; they analyze what went wrong, learn from it, and apply those lessons moving forward. It's this constant cycle of learning that fuels their growth, allowing them to adapt and evolve over time.

Here's how wellness expert Dan De Luis explained it:

> I think it's a little bit of both. I mean, the main part is the lucky part that I got. And then another part is the passion. I didn't have passion for life, you know, and the passion I had was misdirected because of some mental health issues that I had, and I didn't know how to deal with them. But once I started reaching out for help, when I hit that rock bottom, I started to rebuild myself. So, I was born into a situation, but I made myself into who I'm supposed to be.

Everyone wants the biscuit but not the gravy. You see those famous people—the top 1 percent of entrepreneurs, the star athletes, the influencers flaunting their fancy cars, designer clothes, and shiny Rolexes—and it's easy to think they just stumbled into success. It's like people believe they were handed everything on a silver platter with no effort involved. You hear stories about how someone got discovered overnight or got a lucky break, and let me tell you, that's all a bunch of BS. Especially today, with Instagram showcasing the glamorous lives of the "famous," what you see is just the floss. You don't see the challenging climb, the tragedies, the perseverance, or the raw reality of what it takes to get there.

Here's how NFL player Marques Ogden put it:

> Made. I was born with the gift to talk and be a good listener, yes, but being born with something is a talent. I had a God-given talent to speak, to educate, to inspire. But without the training, without going through all the crap, without the life lessons, without going broke, being bankrupt, losing my home, getting divorced, living in an apartment, being out of food, without that, I wouldn't be as good a speaker as I am. I've been made to do this. I had to work my butt off to get to this point. Being born is great. That's awesome. But if you want to be *great*, in my opinion, you've got to make yourself, right? Nobody made me who I am today. I've worked on it. I have people around me, and I've gotten better at my craft every single day, period.

The truth is, not many people get success handed to them—those of us who have made it worked our asses off to get there. We're talking late nights, early mornings, sleepless weeks, and sometimes not even paying ourselves for months on end. It's that "whatever it takes" attitude that drives us. We take the hits, learn from our failures, and keep pushing forward, no holds barred. But nobody talks about that grind. Instead, they romanticize the end result without acknowledging the sweat, tears, and sheer grit it takes to make it happen.

That's the conversation we need to have. It's not just about the flashy cars or the success that looks glamorous from the outside. It's about the relentless work behind the scenes, the sacrifices made, and the mental fortitude required to keep going when the going gets tough. It's time we shine a light on the real story—the truth about how success is earned, not given. The next time you see someone living the dream, remember that it's probably a lot harder than it looks. Behind every success story is a mountain of effort, resilience, and determination that should be celebrated just as much as the triumph itself.

So, are we born or made? Some folks swear by the idea that entrepreneurship is in your genes, like inheriting your grandpa's old watch. They argue that certain individuals are just wired differently from birth, born with an insatiable appetite for risk, an innate creativity that sets them apart, and a natural knack for leadership.

> *"I believe you're born with enthusiasm. You either have it or you don't. I cannot teach enthusiasm. Can I believe that you're born with that entrepreneurial spirit? There are very few people that you can convert. Now, they may have it without realizing it, but guess what... you'll notice it.*
> *They go beyond what you asked for."* ~ Joe Tomarchio of Mr. Tire, Inc. & Monro Muffler

For these born entrepreneurs, it's like they've got a compass in their soul that points them straight to the world of business. They thrive in the face of uncertainty, seeing challenges as opportunities to flex their entrepreneurial muscles and make their mark on the world.

"I think you're made mainly because I think the way that we're born can certainly influence the way that we're wired and our ability to be maybe made in a certain way. But I've seen so many different personalities thrive and survive in entrepreneurship and make it so I don't think you're necessarily born I think you can be made for sure. I think people can I firm confidence that people can change, even though our core wiring may be a certain way, you may think certain ways, but if you're true to yourself, you'll be able to identify your strengths, your weaknesses, and supplement those weaknesses with others that can compliment you know, from that standpoint, so if I had to go with one or the other, I'd probably say made. I think we can choose to be made."

~ Kevin Conway, Professional Racecar Driver (Nascar, Blancpain Super Trofeo Championship, Toyota)

The truth is, I believe you're both born and made. It's a blend of both. Entrepreneurs might come into this world with certain traits that give them an advantage, but it's their experiences—both the good and the bad—that shape those traits into the qualities we respect. It's this combination of inherent qualities and life experiences that creates each individual's unique entrepreneurial DNA. It's the choices we make in between that ultimately determine our outcomes. Being born is just the starting point, and in America, that's only the beginning. Having amazing parents? That's a bonus.

"I think it's both. I was intelligent enough, and I applied myself, you know? So I had a good start. So part of it, you

know, is genetics, DNA, and all that stuff. Partly that, then you can screw it up as well. So you have to sort of keep on the path. And so it's, I think it's a little of both. It's hard to say what makes one person want to, you know, one way and the other person another way. I do believe there's luck involved, too." ~ Max Gottlieb.

Tyler Wagner, an entrepreneur, author, and public speaker, agrees, putting it this way:

I feel like it's a blend of both, and I will explain why. So, I do think as far as what I've become, I think you are born with certain kinds of, just certain elements or whatever you want to call them, that make you different or make you who you are, obviously. I have a natural kind of gift of gab, they call it, or just an outgoing personality, which I think you are born with. And then, as far as being made, I think my environment, and I think about my mom and dad, just everything around me as a child growing up, it makes sense why I am where I am when I think back on just different things that happened and that I saw. It just makes sense that I went this path, I guess you could say.

You've got folks who seem to have all the luck, but if they had any luck at all, it would be bad luck. Then you've got those who can fall out of bed and land on a gold mine. But for the other 99 percent of us, we find ourselves somewhere in the mix of being born or made for success. I was born a salesman—that was my talent right from the get-go. I learned from my wins and losses, and believe me, there were times when I felt defeated. But it was that fire in my belly, that relentless desire to make money, that kept me pushing forward. I looked at my competition and knew I could do it better. So, it was either defeat or inspiration. Lions starve to death if they quit after a loss.

If you take the time to learn about other people's journeys, you'll uncover a treasure trove of insights and inspiration. Most successful folks experience the same ups and downs; the numbers just change. Failing sucks—everyone fails, and I mean everyone. What matters is whether you're willing to get back in the ring and fight again. Many a person has wished they'd taken more chances. If I hadn't taken a chance, I wouldn't have the incredible wife I'm blessed with today.

Invest in yourself—never stop learning. And I'm not just talking about your craft; dive into anything and everything. We have a wealth of knowledge at our fingertips these days. Thirty years ago, finding answers was a challenge, but now it's like shooting fish in a barrel. We're athletes in the arena of mental strength, constantly building ourselves up to pursue our goals. We need to develop that scar tissue. Just like a lion, you've got to get up and hunt every day. You never know when your next meal will come or if it'll be your last.

We entrepreneurs share that same relentless drive. We've got to be ready to seize opportunities when they come knocking. More millionaires are made during downturns than during upturns. The truth is, a lot of people don't have the stomach to take risks, especially after riding a wave of easy times. Good times can make some weak, but they allow others to hone their skills, getting them ready for the next big opportunity.

But here's the kicker: As you accumulate success, it's easy to start protecting what you have. This can lead to complacency and distract you from chasing after those golden opportunities. Remember, one path can lead to easy wins, while the other might bring a serious ass-whooping. One feels good, and the other can hurt like hell. Stay sharp, stay hungry, and don't let comfort cloud your vision.

In a world that often glorifies the "self-made" person, we need to remember that we all stand on the shoulders of those who came before us. Family, mentors, and communities play crucial roles in shaping our journeys. For every entrepreneur who seems to thrive alone, there's a network of support pushing them forward.

Ultimately, the entrepreneurial journey is shaped by both nature and nurture. It's about recognizing your inherent qualities, honing them through experience, and surrounding yourself with those who uplift and challenge you. The willpower to succeed doesn't just come from what you're born with; it's also built through facing and overcoming obstacles.

Hollywood producer Leif Bristow put it this way:

> I think we are definitely born with incredible potential. Sometimes we aren't given the opportunity to understand how to harness our own potential. But I

believe that we're born with an incredible power within us, and sometimes it's not everybody's journey, but sometimes our drive and our vision and our tenacity forces us to step into a path that then becomes what we are made to do, you know? I think success is the pride in knowing that you accomplished what you set out to do in that dream. But most everything in life takes a little bit of luck. It is a benefactor, whether that's a parent, a teacher, a financier, someone who believes in us and gives us those empowering words as we grow, so that we have that tenacity to push. And that luck to me is 90 % hard work. But I think we're born with the aptitude and how we absorb all those messages that come into our lives.

In a similar vein, live painter John Bukaty puts it like this:

I feel like we are born with opportunities. We are born with certain skill sets physically and we are born with opportunities. And the second part of it would be how do you make them come true? How do you paint the image of this beautiful life in your head? How do you execute it? How do you take it into action? How do you embody it? How do you embody your beliefs? How do you integrate the belief system that you now know? That's the hard part. You get the message from spirit or somebody else, and then you have to go do the work. You have to integrate it. That's the integrity. So if you're talking a big game and you're not integrating it, then you have shit for integrity, right?

As you go on your own entrepreneurial adventure, embrace both the qualities you've inherited and the lessons life throws your way. Remember, setbacks are just part of the process. It's how you respond to those challenges that will carve out your path. Be adaptable, learn continuously, and grow—you'll find that the mountains you face become easier to climb with each step forward.

So, what's the takeaway? The entrepreneurial journey is a wild ride marked by resilience, creativity, adaptability, and strong connections. These traits don't just help you succeed in business; they also allow you to make a real impact in your community. Embrace these qualities, and you'll be well on your way to forging your own path and achieving your goals, no matter what obstacles stand in your way.

And remember, it's not just about the glitz and glamour you see on social media. Every successful entrepreneur has put in the hard work and faced their fair share of struggles to get where they are. So, roll up your sleeves, dig in, and don't be afraid to climb those mountains. You've got what it takes!

"There are different kinds of gifts, but the same Spirit distributes them. There are different kinds of service, but the same Lord. There are different kinds of working, but in all of them and in everyone it is the same God at work. Now to each one the manifestation of the Spirit is given for the common good."
~ 1 Corinthians 12:4-7 (NIV) ~

Chapter 11

THE POWER OF
NETWORKING
IN BUSINESS

"As iron sharpens iron, so one person sharpens another."
~ Proverbs 27:17 (NIV) ~

Networking is crucial for business success. It's not just about exchanging business cards; it's about forming genuine connections that can lead to opportunities. Different networking opportunities abound, from industry events to online platforms. To make the most out of every networking chance, focus on authenticity, be open to learning from others, and don't be afraid to ask for help.

The scripture above reminds us that we grow stronger through our relationships, much like how iron sharpens iron. Networking, at its core, is about exchanging knowledge, support, and wisdom. When we surround ourselves with others who can challenge us and help us grow, we not only sharpen our own skills but also contribute to the success of others.

Building relationships in today's ever-changing economy can feel like navigating a minefield. With technology and instant gratification driving the conversation, many folks expect quick service and cheap prices. But here's the kicker: relationships take time to nurture. They're not just a series of transactions; they're like fine wine—better when aged but easily spoiled by a single misstep.

In business, the saying *"It's not what you know, it's who you know"* holds true. I've found that there's rarely anything I can't figure out by knowing someone who knows someone. Over time, sticking with the same industry and community can turn you into a powerhouse. It's the aggregation of marginal gains over the years that leads to success, and then one day, you might just wake up and realize you're a sixty-year-old overnight success, having worked in the same market for twenty-six years.

You know you're making an impact when people mention your name without having met you, hoping it lends them credibility. I used to work for a guy in Texas named Alec, and customers would come in claiming, *"Yeah, I was talking to Alex the other day, and he said I could get a good deal."* We always knew they didn't really know him because they called him "Alex" instead of "Alec." This highlights the importance of genuine connections; if someone is going to vouch for you, they should actually know you.

When you've been in an industry long enough, you become adept at networking. You're constantly figuring out who does what—who can handle sheetrock and paint, who pours concrete, who changes oil, and who handles inspection stickers. The power of networking is really not about trying to get things for free; everybody's gotta make money. It's about making smart deals. I always aim for a fair exchange, knowing that everyone needs to profit.

One of the most powerful aspects of networking is the potential for referrals. A solid network can become a valuable source of business leads. When you build relationships based on trust, people are more likely to refer clients to you. In turn, you should reciprocate by referring business to those within your network, creating a mutually beneficial cycle. This is where collaborations come into play. When businesses work together, they can enhance their offerings and reach a broader audience.

Cultivating relationships is like a marriage: you have to work at it constantly; otherwise, you risk ending up in divorce court. As you get older, this principle becomes even clearer. We're not just trying to get rich quickly; we're playing the long game, building lasting wealth. The same goes for relationships. I've found that solid relationships only get stronger over time.

I've been married to my wife for forty years. It hasn't always been perfect, but after working out the kinks, it's pretty sweet. It's about the long haul. And just like in marriage, sometimes the balance isn't fifty-fifty; it can be ninety-ten. In those meaningful relationships, when you're on the 10 percent, you're benefiting, and when you're on the 90 percent, you're giving back. That's the essence of true connection.

Collaborations can take many forms—joint ventures, co-hosting events, or simply endorsing one another's services. For instance, if you're a contractor, partnering with an interior designer can lead to referrals from both sides, creating a win-win situation. By endorsing each other, you build credibility and expand your reach.

In my experience, people reciprocate when they know you're reliable. If someone needs help closing a property deal, I refer them to my trusted title company and encourage them to mention my name, which adds credibility. But I'm careful about whom I recommend; I won't send someone to a contractor if I'm not confident in their work. A poor referral can damage your own reputation.

By cultivating these relationships and focusing on making solid deals, you create a network that supports your business growth while also helping others succeed. Remember, effective networking is about fostering trust and ensuring everyone involved benefits. Don't just throw names around; be selective and strategic in your referrals. This will strengthen your own standing in the community and build a reputation people can rely on.

Today's fast-paced economy, driven by technology, has led to a desire for instant gratification, which runs counter to the long-term nature of building relationships. The younger generation may want quick results, but the reality is that meaningful connections take time to nurture. While they may learn this later in life, it's essential for all of us to understand that relationships are a two-way street. If you associate with self-serving individuals, you'll likely encounter challenges.

Through my journey, I've discovered that one of my greatest skills is the ability to empathize with others. This realization struck me during a podcast with Dick Marriott from MiTek, during which I recognized that my ability to connect with people on their level was invaluable. Remembering where I came from—starting as a yard dog—helps me relate to everyone, no matter their position. Everyone, from those mowing grass to those crunching numbers, is striving to provide for their families.

Mentors are crucial at every stage of your career. They serve as guidance counselors through the journey of business. Reflecting on my past, I realize I wouldn't be where I am today without the mentors who shaped my path. They don't always have to be formal mentors; sometimes, they're just individuals who offer guidance and support.

I've had three great mentors throughout my career—each distinct but all extremely intelligent. They provided invaluable insights that helped mold me into the businessperson I am today. As we progress in our careers, we must also turn around and become mentors ourselves.

Mentors can also come in the form of negative experiences. A bad boss or coworker can teach you what not to do. Every experience—good or bad—provides a lesson that can guide you in your own leadership style. The most challenging experiences often inspire the most remarkable growth.

Ultimately, what you put in is what you get out. Surround yourself with people who can offer wisdom, and don't hesitate to learn from their mistakes. It's all part of building your empire, and as you navigate this journey, remember that relationships and networking are at the heart of sustainable success. The world may say relationships don't matter in business anymore, but that's a load of crap. You'll learn this the hard way if you don't heed my advice. Being kind to everyone, regardless of their position, will pay off big time.

Cultivating relationships takes time and effort, much like a marriage. Relationships can be easily destroyed by a single bad decision. Building strong connections requires ongoing work; it's not just about immediate gains. The best relationships grow stronger over time, much like my marriage of forty years. While it hasn't always been perfect, working through challenges has made our bond even sweeter.

"Plans fail for lack of counsel,
but with many advisers they succeed."
~ Proverbs 15:22 (NIV) ~

Chapter 12

SELL OR RUN THE COMPANY UNTIL YOU DIE

"Suppose one of you wants to build a tower.
Won't you first sit down and estimate the cost
to see if you have enough money to complete it?"
~ Luke 14:28 (NIV) ~

Just as one must carefully plan and assess the resources before building a tower, entrepreneurs must thoughtfully evaluate their options and the potential consequences of their decisions. As I reflect on my twenty-four-year journey as an entrepreneur, one thing has become clear: the importance of continuous learning. In July 2022, I hired a new general manager with the hope of expanding my facility and improving daily operations. However, I made the mistake of letting go of some control, particularly over financial matters. I thought I was empowering him, but I soon realized I had entrusted my business to someone who prioritized his own interests over the well-being of the team.

Initially, he presented himself as the smartest person in the room, often starting conversations with, *"I'm going to tell you the truth."* I naively went along with it for two years, enduring many challenging conversations and grappling with the loyalty of my long-standing employees. When he ultimately gave his notice, I was devastated. I believed I had hired someone capable of steering Apex in the right direction, but I quickly discovered that he cared more about his title and paycheck than the people in the company.

As he prepared to leave, it became evident he had little regard for anyone but himself. He spoke to only three employees before exiting, leaving the rest in shock. It was then that I realized he had never truly invested in the team or understood their struggles. The loyalty my employees showed me during that time was a stark contrast to his behavior. They revealed that many of them were unhappy, feeling verbally abused and unappreciated.

This experience was a wake-up call. I recognized that I had allowed someone to create a toxic environment, and I felt a deep sense of disappointment in myself for not catching it sooner. My empathy, which I have always viewed as one of my greatest strengths, reminded me that everyone, regardless of their position, is just trying to provide for their families and do their best.

One employee shared a poignant visual: He lowered his hands to demonstrate how he felt diminished under the previous management. This moment reinforced the value of connecting with people on their level, something I had learned from my own humble beginnings as a yard dog. I realized I was more than capable of fostering an environment where everyone felt valued and understood.

As I consider my future, I have come to a decisive conclusion: I will either sell the business or run it until I die, but I will never let someone else take the reins again unless I can train them from a young age. The lessons learned through years of struggle have molded me into the leader I am today. I want to ensure that, if something were to happen to me, my wife Sheryl and my team would know how to keep the company thriving. I always trusted them and would want them to trust each other in my absence.

Ultimately, the journey of entrepreneurship is fraught with challenges, but these trials shape us into who we are meant to be. I hope to share these lessons with my grandchildren, teaching them that every role is significant, no matter how small. It's about the connections we build and the values we uphold, ensuring everyone is recognized for their contributions.

"Let your eyes look straight ahead, fix your gaze directly before you. Give careful thought to the paths for your feet and be steadfast in all your ways. Do not turn to the right or the left; keep your foot from evil."
~ Proverbs 4:25-27 (NIV) ~

Chapter 13

REFLECTING ON
MY JOURNEY

*"Brothers and sisters, I do not consider myself yet to have taken hold of it.
But one thing I do: Forgetting what is behind and straining toward what
is ahead, I press on toward the goal to win the prize for which God has
called me heavenward in Christ Jesus."*
~ Philippians 3:13-14 (NIV) ~

Where am I now? I find myself at what feels like the pinnacle of my life. While I continue striving for more, I'm truly satisfied if this is as good as it gets. My days are filled with a wide variety of activities—podcasting, cold plunges, sauna workouts, fasting, and even car racing. I'm deeply engaged in the truss manufacturing business and will soon take on the role of president of the national trade association.

Just as the apostle Paul pressed forward toward his goal, I, too, continue to move forward, never fully satisfied with what lies behind me but always striving to grow, learn, and achieve more. Life has become a rich mosaic of continuous learning and doing. Whether I'm managing our family farm, renovating a house, or squeezing in writing amidst a packed workout and reading schedule, there's never a dull moment. I enjoy designing furniture, building fountains from scratch, and mastering fence construction. Each day brings new lessons, ensuring I'm continually growing.

I relish spending hours bush-hogging vast acres or fishing in my fully stocked five-acre pond. At work, I'm fortunate to have a competent general manager running Apex, which allows me to focus on future growth. But make no mistake—success doesn't grant you the luxury of complacency. The landscape of business and governance is ever-changing, and staying vigilant is essential.

I embrace experimentation, like undergoing an eighty-two-hour fast, to keep life exhilarating. My eight grandchildren, each with diverse interests ranging from sports to music, add a lively spark to my days. Racing has become a thrilling new hobby. While I'm not yet racing wheel-to-wheel, I'm training for my license and looking forward to future events, including one in Miami. Owning a one-hundred-eighty-two-acre farm has introduced me to the joys and challenges of raising cattle, including a rare bull whose lineage mirrors the uniqueness of my own life.

Life is not without its risks—managing cattle has taught me the unpredictable nature of farming, yet witnessing the miracle of life unfolding in the pasture never ceases to amaze me.

Amidst these personal pursuits, my role as a mentor and coach to aspiring entrepreneurs has become increasingly central. I guide them through the complexities of starting and growing their businesses, drawing on my extensive experience to help them navigate the often turbulent waters of entrepreneurship. This mentorship goes beyond mere business advice; I focus on fostering their resilience, adaptability, and holistic well-being, preparing them for the psychological demands of entrepreneurship as much as the strategic challenges.

Additionally, I am expanding my horizons as an author, with plans to write more books that explore the depths of entrepreneurial spirit, personal growth, and the pivotal experiences that shape our paths. Each page I write is a step toward understanding and sharing the complexities of life's journey.

I'm incredibly grateful for the life I've built. From cherishing the unique joys each of my three adult children brings into my life to maintaining a daily connection with my brother, these relationships form my foundation. I've been blessed with a wonderful forty-year marriage rooted in love and persistence since our serendipitous meeting at a football game.

Looking back, I realize my life is more than I could have ever asked for. Despite the struggles of my early years, my journey has been one of immense growth and happiness. I am content and at peace with my accomplishments, yet eager for what the future holds. While I dream of one day owning a private jet, my life is already rich with experiences and love—a testament to the rewards of perseverance, passion, and the deep satisfaction that comes from guiding others on their paths to success.

As I close this chapter of my book, I hope my stories inspire you to embrace your challenges with courage and view every day as an opportunity to write your own narrative of fulfillment and achievement.

"I will remember the deeds of the Lord; yes, I will remember your miracles of long ago. I will consider all your works and meditate on all your mighty deeds."
~ Psalm 77:11-12 (NIV) ~

ARE WE BORN OR MADE?

"Yet you, Lord, are our Father. We are the clay,
you are the potter; we are all the work of your hand."
~ Isaiah 64:8 (NIV) ~

As we reach the end of this journey through the entrepreneurial landscape, it's time to reflect on the question that has guided us: Are we born or made? The answer is not black and white; it's a rich blend of both nature and nurture, shaped by experiences, choices, and the unwavering commitment to grow.

Just as the potter shapes the clay, we, too, are shaped by our experiences and the choices we make along the way. Throughout this book, we've explored the fundamental principles that define successful entrepreneurs—their integrity, resilience, and relentless pursuit of knowledge. We've seen how the power of networking can open doors and how cultivating meaningful relationships lays the groundwork for lasting success. You don't just build a business; you build a community.

It's important to recognize that every entrepreneur's path is unique. Some may possess innate qualities that drive them, but those traits alone won't guarantee success. What truly sets entrepreneurs apart is their willingness to learn, adapt, and overcome obstacles. It's about the effort you put in when no one is watching, the sacrifices made during the toughest times, and the mindset that keeps you moving forward despite setbacks.

Reflecting on my own journey, I've experienced the highs and lows, the lessons learned from mistakes, and the joys of guiding others. The entrepreneurship landscape is ever-changing, demanding a solid foundation of skills and the ability to pivot and embrace new challenges. It's about recognizing how growth often comes from discomfort and true fulfillment lies in leaving a legacy of kindness, integrity, and support for future generations.

As you consider your own entrepreneurial journey, ask yourself this: What legacy do you want to leave? How will you impact those around you—your team, your community, your family? The path to success is not just about financial gain; it's about the relationships you build and the lives you touch along the way.

In the end, whether you believe we are born with the qualities of a leader or are made through our experiences, remember this: The journey of entrepreneurship is a continuous evolution. Each setback can be a stepping stone, each relationship a potential collaboration, and each day an opportunity to write your own story.

So, as you move forward, embrace the challenges, stay true to your values, and never underestimate the power of hard work and perseverance. You have the potential to shape your destiny and the lives of others, proving that in the world of entrepreneurship, we are indeed both born and made.

"For I know the plans I have for you," declares the Lord,
"plans to prosper you and not to harm you,
plans to give you a hope and a future."
~ Jeremiah 29:11 (NIV) ~

ACKNOWLEDGMENTS

I would first like to give special acknowledgment to my parents, Larry and Penny Dix, for their unwavering support, for always seeing the positive in me, and for always making me and my brother Richard number one in their lives.

To my wonderful wife of forty years, Sheryl, thanks for putting up with me all these years. Who would've thought that October 22, 1983, would be the day that changed my life forever? Your unwavering love and belief in me have been my anchor and the gift of allowing me to be me. I love you forever.

To my three amazing children, Joshua, Kelsey, and Jared, and my eight beautiful grandchildren, you are my greatest pride. I hope this book inspires you to embrace your own journeys and understand the importance of hard work, integrity, and leaving a legacy. I hope you understand why I have this unwavering passion for these principles.

A special thanks to Bridgetta Tomarchio, whose guidance and mentorship were instrumental in bringing this book to life. Your insights helped me navigate the writing process effectively. Thank you for believing in this project!

ABOUT THE AUTHOR

Larry Dix is a seasoned entrepreneur with decades of experience navigating the highs and lows of the business world. From overcoming early financial struggles to scaling multiple ventures, Larry's journey is a testament to the power of resilience, grit, and faith. He has built businesses from the ground up, turning setbacks into stepping stones, and has guided others through the toughest challenges of entrepreneurship.

Larry's mission is simple: to inspire, educate, and empower the next generation of entrepreneurs. Through his popular *Born or Made Podcast*, Larry interviews top industry leaders, sharing their wisdom and success strategies with listeners worldwide. His podcast dives deep into the mindset, habits, and principles that drive top performers, with a focus on actionable insights that entrepreneurs can apply to their own businesses.

In addition to his podcast, Larry is a sought-after speaker and coach, helping entrepreneurs unlock their full potential and scale their businesses. With a wealth of hard-won experience, he provides practical guidance, expert advice, and the mental tools necessary to succeed in today's competitive landscape. Larry's next chapter includes writing future books that continue to inspire entrepreneurs on their journey, guiding them toward not just business success but personal growth and fulfillment.

Larry's work is rooted in a belief that true success is built on faith, perseverance, and a commitment to lifelong learning. Through his speaking, coaching, and writing, he continues to equip entrepreneurs with the skills they need to not just survive but thrive.

www.bornormadepodcast.com/